COMPETENCY-BASED EDUCATION IGNITED

A TRANSFORMATIONAL SYSTEMWIDE APPROACH FOR LEADERS

RICHARD A. DELORENZO
ROXANNE L. MOURANT

Foreword by Robert J. Marzano

Solution Tree | Press

a division of
Solution Tree

555 North Morton Street
Bloomington, IN 47404
800.733.6786 (toll free) / 812.336.7700
FAX: 812.336.7790

email: info@SolutionTree.com
SolutionTree.com

Visit **go.SolutionTree.com/leadership** to download the free reproducible in this book.

Printed in the United States of America

FSC
www.fsc.org
MIX
Paper from responsible sources
FSC® C008955

Library of Congress Cataloging-in-Publication Data

Names: DeLorenzo, Richard A., author. | Mourant, Roxanne L., author.
Title: Competency-based education ignited : a transformational systemwide approach for leaders / Richard A. DeLorenzo, Roxanne L. Mourant.
Description: Bloomington, IN : Solution Tree Press, 2024. | Includes bibliographical references and index.
Identifiers: LCCN 2024003809 (print) | LCCN 2024003810 (ebook) | ISBN 9781960574022 (paperback) | ISBN 9781960574039 (ebook)
Subjects: LCSH: Competency-based education—United States.
Classification: LCC LC1032 .D45 2024 (print) | LCC LC1032 (ebook) | DDC 370.110973—dc23/eng/20240226

LC record available at https://lccn.loc.gov/2024003809

LC ebook record available at https://lccn.loc.gov/2024003810

Solution Tree
Jeffrey C. Jones, CEO
Edmund M. Ackerman, President

Solution Tree Press
President and Publisher: Douglas M. Rife
Associate Publishers: Todd Brakke and Kendra Slayton
Editorial Director: Laurel Hecker
Art Director: Rian Anderson
Copy Chief: Jessi Finn
Senior Production Editor: Miranda Addonizio
Proofreader: Charlotte Jones
Cover Designer: Rian Anderson
Acquisitions Editors: Carol Collins and Hilary Goff
Content Development Specialist: Amy Rubenstein
Associate Editors: Sarah Ludwig and Elijah Oates
Editorial Assistant: Anne Marie Watkins

ACKNOWLEDGMENTS

CBE Ignited would like to thank the following: Mary and Bob Rubadeau; Jessica Enderson; all the students and staff who helped on our journey; Barbara DeLorenzo; and the Educating for Leadership board members for their review, insights, and support.

Solution Tree Press would like to thank the following reviewers:

Lindsey Bingley
Literacy and Numeracy Lead
Foothills Academy Society
Calgary, Alberta, Canada

Benjamin J. Kitslaar
Principal
West Side Elementary School
Elkhorn, Wisconsin

Jennifer Steele
Assistant Director, Athletics and Activities
Fort Smith Public Schools
Fort Smith, Arkansas

Kim Timmerman
Principal
ADM Middle School
Adel, Iowa

Ringnolda Jofee' Tremain
Director of Professional Learning
Texas Leadership Public Schools
Arlington, Texas

Visit **go.SolutionTree.com/leadership** to download the free reproducible in this book.

"All the darkness in the world cannot extinguish the light of a single candle."

—Saint Francis of Assisi

TABLE OF CONTENTS

Reproducible page is in italics.

CHAPTER 3

CHAPTER 4

CHAPTER 5

ABOUT THE AUTHORS

Richard A. DeLorenzo is the pioneering force behind the inception of CBE Ignited, having earned international recognition for his leadership in education and organizational restructuring. Renowned for his holistic grassroots methodology, he has carved a niche in reinventing school systems to cater to the diverse needs of learners. Notably, his stewardship led Alaska's Chugach School District to pioneer the transition from a time-based to a performance-based educational paradigm, where students are required to achieve performance benchmarks rather than accumulate credits for graduation.

In a career spanning decades, Richard has demonstrated a profound commitment to working with marginalized youth and students with disabilities across various education landscapes. Revered as a visionary, he possesses a remarkable capacity to enlist others in his vision for advancing the education landscape. Beyond the borders of the United States, he has lent his expertise to numerous organizations worldwide. His account of a historically challenged rural district achieving remarkable progress in student achievement through competency-based education (CBE) earned the distinction of being one of the inaugural education recipients of the esteemed Malcolm Baldrige National Quality Award.

Since 2018, Richard has been instrumental in reshaping the Russian education system, particularly in Moscow, where he orchestrated the transformation of thousands of schools toward personalized learning models, catalyzing positive implications for the nation's economic future. His desire for scaling CBE knows no bounds, as he remains steadfast in aiding nations committed to fostering enhanced educational systems.

Richard's academic journey includes a bachelor's degree in education and special education from Central Washington University, followed by a master's degree in special education and educational administration from the University of Alaska

Juneau. He furthered his credentials by obtaining a superintendent certification from the University of Alaska Anchorage.

To learn more about Richard's work, visit https://cbeignited.org/team or follow him on LinkedIn (www.linkedin.com/in/richard-delorenzo-7165684).

Roxanne L. Mourant, MEd, is chief education officer of Educating for Leadership, Inc., in Alaska. She is a former education consultant with the Re-Inventing Schools Coalition (RISC), where she was part of a team that led system change through leadership, curricular improvement, and professional development initiatives and aligned those efforts with the district's progress as a competency-based system. Roxy has been an educator since 1987 with background as a robotics coach, teacher, and school and district administrator in a variety of school settings. Her educational experiences range from working in a predominantly low-income minority school to working in some of the most affluent and high-performing schools. She has also taught graduate courses on leadership and curriculum for the University of Alaska and Alaska Pacific University as an adjunct faculty member.

She has presented throughout the United States on topics ranging from developing a culture of high expectations to implementing support systems for students who are struggling academically and behaviorally. She has also worked with educational leaders to make curricula more relevant to minority students.

Roxy received a bachelor's degree in education from Alaska Pacific University and a master's degree in educational technology in teaching from Ashford University in Iowa.

To book Richard or Roxanne for professional development, contact pd@SolutionTree.com.

FOREWORD

By Robert J. Marzano

When the history of the development of competency-based education (CBE) in the United States is written, Richard A. DeLorenzo's name will be in the first chapter. I first met him in the late 1990s after Chugach School District in Alaska had already developed an award-winning, comprehensive CBE system under Rich's direction and leadership. He actually called me to describe what the district had done, and, to be honest, it sounded too good to be true. My doubts were quelled when I had a chance to visit the district about a year later. Without exaggeration, it completely changed my way of thinking about K–12 schooling. After that, I had the good fortune of working with Rich and the organization he created (the Re-Inventing Schools Coalition [RISC]) for a number of years, which ultimately led me to the place of being one of the many laborers in the orchard of developing and promoting CBE systems. *Competency-Based Education Ignited*, by DeLorenzo and his coauthor, Roxanne L. Mourant, is a welcome addition to the growing line of resources available to those schools and districts interested in CBE.

In the book, DeLorenzo and Mourant address many of the same topics that other CBE texts address. These topics include shared vision, school culture, the utilization of standards, grading and reporting, grouping and regrouping, and the flexible use of time. Like those other books, *CBE Ignited* offers many practical steps districts, schools, and individual teachers can take relative to those topics. But unlike other books, *CBE Ignited* seeks to elucidate the change in basic assumptions and beliefs required by administrators, teachers, students, and parents to implement an effective CBE system. This is definitely one of the more powerful aspects of the book since some of these assumptions and beliefs represent a veritable sea change. Various assumptions and beliefs addressed in the book include:

- Students should have a voice and choice in how they learn and how they are assessed
- Codes of conduct should be created jointly by teachers and students

- The curriculum students are expected to master should be completely transparent at all grade levels and in all subject areas
- Students should move to the next higher level of content as soon as they are ready
- Students should not move on to a higher level of content until they have demonstrated mastery at their current level of content
- The minimum GPA to graduate from high school should be a 3.0
- A high school diploma should be a guarantee of mastery of specific knowledge and skills

In keeping with this emphasis on shifting assumptions and beliefs, the authors continually contrast the CBE approach with the traditional approach, so much so that by the end of the book, the reader is clear as to the differences between these two methods of schooling. One can make the case that this outcome alone is worth the price of the book.

One overarching structure in the book is the authors' CBE road map to implementation, which contains six stages: (1) awareness, (2) readiness, (3) first implementation, (4) routine, (5) refinement, and (6) replication. Following these stages truly provides the reader with a process that takes them from their initial attempts to learn about CBE to a system that has been field-tested, refined, and operated in a continuous improvement mode.

Also of note is the authors' introduction of the concept of third-order change, which adds a new dimension to the theory base on change. According to the authors, third-order change occurs when the change itself creates a new culture that is easily scalable, again emphasizing the importance of changing assumptions and beliefs along with structures and protocols.

Finally, one should not minimize the wealth of knowledge and experience accrued by the first author from his two-year project to transform the education system in Russia, during which time he actually took up residence there. This experiential base is unprecedented in the world of CBE. I know of no person other than Rich who can talk about and provide experiential guidance relative to changing the system of schooling in an entire country, an idea that still inspires me even by the simple act of writing this sentence.

I used to think that CBE was the inevitable future, but I now think that CBE has broken down the door to the present. It's probably safe to say that in some form, CBE is being implemented in every U.S. state. Those involved in these implementations are to be commended for their vision and commitment, but they should also be wary of the many pitfalls that are ever present when effecting this type of change. Present-day implementers should learn firsthand from the schools and districts that have already begun the CBE journey and read widely from the growing body of books on the topic. One of those books they should definitely read is *CBE Ignited* by DeLorenzo and Mourant.

INTRODUCTION

Creating a New Vision for Student-Centered Schools

Every student has a unique destiny. Schools need to provide the conditions and support necessary to help students find their paths in life. To do this, they can't rely on the traditional way that schools have been run for generations; they must reinvent themselves by placing students at the center of their learning and giving them the tools and opportunities to master all the skills, knowledge, and content that they need for lifelong success.

In 1994, Richard was a partner in an educational team that set out to dramatically change how schools operate in a rural district in Alaska. The genesis of the groundbreaking work we describe in this book began in his classroom a decade earlier in his role as a teacher of students with special needs. He experienced futile frustration with how the traditional system continually failed the majority of students, especially those who didn't fit the typical mold of "normal" students. The deck is stacked significantly against those most in need of personalized and targeted pathways to learning. A significant percentage of all our students are not adequately engaged, struggle in isolation to meet teachers' daily expectations, and ultimately experience chronic failure (Gradient Learning, 2023).

Competency-based education (CBE), also known as proficiency- or standards-based education, creates a new vision for schools and expanded learning classrooms to respond effectively to the educational goals and aptitudes of each student. CBE is student centered, creates a focus on continual progress, and documents within a robust online assessment platform the demonstration of clearly articulated skills and competencies for each student. CBE offers an alternative to failure by promoting learners' confidence and resilience through systems of continuous support until they reach and demonstrate competency. Conversely, students who excel in the classroom have the freedom to move at an accelerated pace.

Educators in a CBE system ask what they want their graduates to know and be able to do and then collectively backward engineer the road map for each student.

The road map includes content that students need to master, learning goals, personalized instructional delivery, meaningful assessments, and transparent reporting of their progress. As educators struggle to meet the diverse needs of their students, the traditional way that schools provide education is becoming more and more untenable. Our goal with this book is to present CBE Ignited as the best approach to address this problem—one that any school can use.

This approach to learning usually begins with good traditional teaching and then shifts into giving students more voice and choice in their learning. In a mature CBE system, students will create, deploy, and navigate their own learning, thereby preparing them in a more relevant manner to manage their future. CBE has four main elements.

1. **A clear scope and sequence:** The knowledge and skills that students need to master (what educators want students to learn and the targets they must reach) are evident and accessible by students.
2. **Proficiency scales:** Each learning target is broken down by a proficiency scale, a learning progression that describes the levels of rigor. For example, on a four-point scale, 1 indicates awareness (understanding with help), a score of 2 indicates readiness (willingness to try with help), a score of 3 indicates routine (meeting the target), and a score of 4 indicates advanced (exceeding expectations).
3. **Student-centered instructional delivery:** Instruction is self-paced and personalized to the learner. Teachers provide the what, but students' voice and choice help dictate when and how they learn.
4. **Assessments that measure and report progress:** Teachers in a CBE system work with students to assess their learning based on skills or competencies. Once students have mastered a competency, they can move on to the next level. Students always know where they are on learning any given skill, and they always know where they're going.

CBE Ignited is a call to action for shifting the traditional time-based educational system to a customized learning model, in which students progress at their own pace based on their mastery of specific competencies. The CBE Ignited approach also relies on a robust digital platform that allows students and teachers to keep track of current learning levels and compare them to the competencies they're striving for. The digital platform consists of different "playlists" of specific strategies for each subject. Artificial intelligence (AI) is embedded in the software to continually assist students by supporting their individual learning styles, continually monitoring their progress, and making suggestions to help them stay on pace. This approach is the answer to our ailing education system because it puts students at the center of their learning and provides them with the tools and processes to be empowered learners.

How Can Readers Use This Book?

The intent of this book is to guide leaders who recognize the current system needs to dramatically change and to provide a road map of what specifically they can do to begin this journey. In transforming your schools, there are many moving pieces held in place by traditional norms and values that making significant change seems almost impossible. We want leaders to have a deep understanding of what the critical components are and to provide tools and processes to help them begin their journey. We start the book off in chapter 1 with a discussion of the struggles that the realm of education is facing in the postpandemic world and the flaws in the traditional system that CBE is poised to fix. Then, in chapter 2, we provide an overview of CBE, its key elements and benefits, the critical steps that schools and districts need to take before implementing CBE, and some success stories. Chapters 3–6 each focus on a key stakeholder, beginning with students and ending with superintendents. Then, we conclude with a look at how CBE can scale up to shift education in the right direction.

Each chapter is structured around essential questions; the stakeholder chapters then present a road map for each stakeholder group to help guide those who are committed. The road map is a proven process that schools can follow.

Transforming the current system to a competency-based system requires a collective vision for serving the educational needs of all students. Courageous stakeholders, including educators, parents, students, policymakers, and business leaders, need to roll up their sleeves and create pathways for students to demonstrate the knowledge, skills, and aptitudes required for success in their future.

What Is the Student Experience During a Typical Day at a CBE School?

Michelle is a seventh-grade student who is often not engaged in her schoolwork and often questions the relevance of the content she is learning. She finds herself jumping through hoops to maintain her grades and not get into trouble, and she has little commitment to most of the content presented to her other than to pass the next test. She must spend a lot of her time taking care of her younger brothers and sisters; her parents both work long hours as money is tight. Because of these factors, she has struggled with school in the past. But things are different this year.

Michelle attends a middle school within a competency-based system that supports and personalizes her educational journey. This school embraces a growth mindset and provides a safe and supportive environment where all students find their own measure of success. Michelle feels this system is more about helping her be successful in life rather than just passing the next test. Michelle knows exactly where she is going in every content area and has a digital personal profile that gives her all the information she needs to help her succeed with her learning. She has been placed in her own instructional levels of competency in each of her core subject areas. Besides embracing a proficiency-based learning environment, this school encourages real-life projects and off-campus experiential learning opportunities to demonstrate what she has mastered.

Michelle's typical school day unfolds like this. Once she wakes up in the morning, she opens her laptop to view her personal digital platform. This platform gives her a quick overview of her current performance levels in all her core subjects, plus her wellness or personal social development levels. Each of these elements has a personal pull-down menu that she can customize. The pull-down menu gives her current detailed information on what she needs to learn and a choice of strategies to move forward. Michelle can make changes to her playlist in real time. Changes can include what she is actively learning as well as how she will be able to demonstrate her mastery of a skill. She can choose to learn independently, with a partner, or in teams. She can choose texts, videos, real-time tutorials, or even virtual assistance from a cloud service tutor to help her when she has questions. She looks over her playlists to see current levels of progression and projected learning rates that correspond in real time with future goals.

Michelle then sets her daily goals and gets ready to catch the bus. Similar to traditional schools, she has a daily schedule and attends class with her peers. However, the critical difference is that she knows exactly where she is on a performance scale in every subject area and what she still needs to do to progress. She has a transparent road map that tracks her progress using current data or real-time feedback. Michelle has clear strategies on how she can progress in her studies with or without a teacher. She uses her time in school to collaborate with her peers and get extra support from her teachers. In English class, she chooses to spend her time reading a novel to prepare for a book study and then attends a brief conference with her teacher. In geometry, she works with a group to better understand how to find the area of triangles while the teacher checks in. Each of her teachers reinforces the appropriate current tools at hand and explores added processes students can use. Options available may offer small-group or one-on-one support when there is an identified gap in the students' learning. The teachers use their own digital platform to monitor and communicate with students about their individual level of competency. Michelle is able to access multiple resources via the web that will provide energy and enthusiasm for the targeted question and open additional opportunities for exploration.

Michelle owns her learning and has the technology, assessment tools, and processes in place to constantly check and adjust daily achievement targets. Michelle may have once struggled in a traditional classroom where a group lecture format and time restricted exposure to limited content prior to a final high-stakes test. Allowing all students their role as the centerpiece of an individualized learning strategy preempts any opportunity to be disillusioned and disappointed in their daily efforts to meet their personal goals in life. Students and their support network of teachers, family, and community-based enrichment programs are all engaged stakeholders in the future success of each and every student.

The Dead Ends and Blind Alleys of Achieving Student Success

The messy part is in the details of student accomplishment because there are so many traditional and illogical barriers that actually hinder the progress of our students within the rigid context of traditional school progressions. Yet, the system will defend these antiquated practices only because it's all they know. My daughter had been in a CBE system when she, at fourteen, entered ninth grade in a different, traditional school district. She had already mastered and proven competencies in the course syllabus requirements to garner enough traditional high school credits to be considered a junior in high school. However, this district's policy prescribed that students can only earn credits for high school–level courses beginning with ninth grade. My daughter was devastated that her hard work would not be recognized in this new setting. She would have to spend the next school year doing the curriculum all over again. This is a classic example of where the system hinders and discourages our students by preserving policies, once well intentioned, that are far past their time of usefulness. Fortunately, my daughter's district backed down once we petitioned for a policy change on behalf of all students who could demonstrate competencies in well-established alternative settings and won the decision.

—RICHARD A. DELORENZO

CHAPTER 1

The Reality That Educators Face

Educational reform initiatives since the 1970s have primarily worked within the current structure of the public education system, which is characterized by grade levels, time-based schedules, and academic calendars. If students do not meet the expectations for achievement within a set time frame, they often experience failure.

Schools and entire districts have launched multiple initiatives to increase opportunities for student success, including adopting new curricula, technologies, and instructional strategies. Despite extensive professional development to support strategies to increase academic achievement coupled with the fierce and creative commitment of highly qualified and engaged educators, significant gaps in learning between student demographic populations persist. Simply stated, our traditional education system builds in the possibility of failure for a large and growing percentage of students.

Before exploring the solution to the problem, it's necessary to fully understand the reality that educators currently face. This chapter answers the following essential questions.

- How has the current traditional system failed to deliver on the promise of success for all students?
- How have we addressed the challenge to revamp and improve our broken system?
- What has the pandemic revealed about the broken educational system?
- What are the takeaways from this chapter?

How Has the Traditional System Failed to Deliver on the Promise of Success for *All* Students?

In 1983, the U.S. Department of Education report, *A Nation at Risk*, sounded an early alarm (National Commission on Excellence in Education, 1983). U.S. K–12 students were falling markedly behind other developed nations. But despite billions of dollars of spending since then, the U.S. education system does not have anything to show for it. There is a breakdown in our education system that has created a crisis in student achievement.

Five years after the passage of No Child Left Behind legislation in 2002, 28 percent of schools failed to meet proficiency goals (Chen, 2023). Four years later, in 2011, the U.S. secretary of education, Arne Duncan, told Congress that the school failure rate could be expected to rise to 82 percent (Parsons, 2011). Education leaders across the country reacted by instituting even more shortsighted teaching-for-testing measures: more high-stakes, expensive tests requiring mandated curricular compliance. Yet in 2017, at the abandonment of the national reporting program, a full one-third of lower-income eighth graders could not demonstrate even minimal competence in reading and mathematics (Stevens, 2020).

The National Assessment of Educational Progress (NAEP), the U.S. educational performance report card, released new and startling statistics in 2023. The average score in history from the 2022 assessment was nine points lower than the average score in 2014. The scores first began declining in 2014, and in total, just 13 percent of eighth graders performed at or above the proficient level, two points lower than in 2018, when barely 15 percent reached the proficient level (National Center for Education Statistics [NCES], n.d.a). Most troubling, according to officials, was the rise in students scoring at or below basic on the exam: 40 percent of eighth graders scored below basic compared to 34 percent in 2018 (Ly, 2023).

An overwhelming majority of states saw significant score declines among fourth and eighth graders in mathematics and reading between 2019 and 2022, with students posting the largest score declines ever recorded in mathematics, according to federal data that provide the most comprehensive evaluation to date of our efforts to focus on academic achievement (NCES, n.d.a, n.d.b). According to NAEP results, between two-thirds and three-quarters of students fail to reach proficiency annually in reading and mathematics, basic skills that are necessary for success in life (NCES, n.d.a, n.d.b). The reality is that as of 2023, students are performing worse than they were decades earlier; for example, scores of lower-performing students in mathematics are at levels last seen in the 1970s (Camera, 2023). This means that millions of students may still be attending our schools but are not performing at a level necessary to master the most fundamental and essential of educational goals.

When compared with other nations, the declines in the United States come into sharp relief. In 2018, U.S. students placed twenty-fifth in the Programme for International Student Assessment (PISA), which is a triennial survey of fifteen-year-old students around the world (FactsMaps, n.d.; Organisation for Economic Co-operation and Development [OECD], 2019). Notably, other nations such as China, Japan, Singapore, and Canada score well above the United States in this ranking (FactsMaps, n.d). The survey assesses the extent to which all students have acquired the necessary skills for full participation in their country's society.

What happens to all these students whose scores don't measure up? They often still graduate, but they do so often unprepared for college and the workforce. Data show that 80 percent of high school seniors obtain a diploma, but less than half of those young adults can proficiently read or complete mathematics problems (Lynch, 2016). In ten states, a student can earn sufficient mathematics credits to gain a graduate diploma but still fall short of meeting the necessary requirements for entry into a state university (Gewertz, 2018).

While the majority of struggling students do still graduate, the dropout rate remains a concern. According to the NCES (2023), in 2021, the status dropout rate for sixteen- to twenty-four-year-olds in the United States was 5.2 percent. While this rate has declined since 2010, this still means that about two million young adults in that age group were not enrolled in school or in receipt of a high school credential (NCES, 2023). The truth is that those unsuccessful students will likely leave school behind forever and struggle in the workforce economy. Failure is evident for underperforming students and results in numbers that will eventually cripple our welfare, health care, prison, and low-income-economic-support systems.

Forty years after *A Nation at Risk*, the question remains: Have we significantly improved education for all students? An article by Dana Goldstein (2019) in *The New York Times* highlights that despite billions of dollars in spending, two-thirds of our students are not proficient in reading. New paradigms are often created by the desperation of an organization to simply survive and then find the missing ingredients necessary to thrive.

We are outraged that the wealthiest country in the world fails to produce better learning results that lead to a full and enriched life for all our citizens. Yet our schools, despite their enormous promise to identify and effect change, continue to operate pretty much the same way they did hundreds of years ago.

Confronting this brutal reality of being stuck in outdated delivery models with arbitrary high-stakes assessments is the first step the United States must take as a nation if leaders want to radically alter the future. The second step is to find acceptable systemic solutions to this crisis. This is why shifting toward a personalized learning model that eliminates the need for high-stakes assessments should be at the core of the solution. This book is designed to bring hope to those educators, parents, businesspeople, politicians, and students who have been frustrated with how the current system fails to deliver on the promise of a high-functioning public education system that provides pathways to success for all students.

Concerned individuals, stakeholders, and educational practitioners must realize together that the historical one-size-fits-all approach to learning in our country's past needs a dramatic overhaul. We need to understand that every student is unique and learns in a different way and at varying rates. We also need to understand as a core value that students must feel safe and connected to the learning environment and to those around them in new and inspiring ways. Our educational system must discover the magic spell that will unleash the dreams and potential of every student in every school. Our system must operate to fulfill the unquestionable mandate that meets the needs of each and every student in our classrooms and prepares them for our nation's future. We can no longer use the tools of our forefathers to prepare for the challenges to come.

During his time teaching in general classrooms, Richard witnessed a destructive pattern of failure empowered by an antiquated and unresponsive system that requires teachers to cover the prescribed subject material, whether students learned it or not. Teachers operating under strict time constraints will hurry on to the next chapter on a prescribed timeline, which only compounds students' sense of confusion, failure, and defeat. Students' daily learning opportunities become focused on doing what's necessary to pass a test; their brains quickly crowd out that content in favor of often unrelated knowledge for the next test. Much of the content offered has little or no linked meaning without the creative umbrella of all the relevant context of the entire learning experience. This is only one of the many disconnecting features of our present delivery system that results in high rates of unengaged students (Gradient Learning, 2023) and millions of students who have given up and dropped out (NCES, 2023).

In talking with thousands of successful students who have shared their experiences with us, we've learned that their main motivation is often not about learning the lesson at hand but to figure out how to earn an A in the class as a whole. They readily admit they are only gaming the system for the letter grades because that is what matters to their parents and the universities they apply to. Richard's conversations with students tend to probe further to ask them to recall a time when they experienced authentic or meaningful learning; students quickly brighten up and describe a certain teacher who made that lesson interesting and added connected content to what mattered most to them. Students often go on to describe projects that helped them understand difficult and complex concepts that they would not ordinarily embrace or fully understand. These learners also volunteer that the more interesting projects from their portfolios have included an active "voice and choice" in the design of the lesson, its content, and how it will be assessed. When asked how often this type of learning occurs in their daily school lives, they lament that it is usually less than 1 percent of their time in the school day.

Conversely, teachers are tasked with doing the best they can but find themselves overwhelmed with arbitrary demands to meet expectations of high-stakes assessment tools, while meeting the emotional and social needs of their students. Personal technology has exacerbated the problem in traditional schools where the simple solution is often to ban these devices. Ironically, technology has created a completely new world of opportunity in terms of rapidly changing platforms of ingenuity in how students acquire knowledge, communicate, entertain themselves, solve problems, and find their place in society.

Schools struggle with a fledgling capacity to adapt readily and quickly to new technology, which results in missing unique opportunities to leverage radical and innovative new technologies to support student learning in a more efficient, effective, and meaningful way.

Students are faced with a completely different world than the one that existed when current adults were students, in terms of both personal trauma and societal pressures. In addition, students need a different skill set to be able to adapt, find happiness, and still thrive economically. Schools need to be agile, flexible, and adaptable to the new realities, but unfortunately our institutions are suffocating under the burden of the traditional, "old school" reality. For example, AI tools such as ChatGPT, which generates text, have been seen by some educational theorists as the next threat to traditional classrooms. The fear is students will simply use this software to generate reasonably good essays to meet requirements in many of their classes. ChatGPT didn't exist until 2022, but immediately schools were scrambling to adjust to the AI phenomenon. We fear this will result in a lengthy discourse, resulting in another lost opportunity to embrace the technology of the world our students will inherit.

Many high school and university graduates will already tell you that current schools just don't prepare them for the real world as they see it (XQ Institute, n.d.). Our nation's public schools, with political school boards, tenuous funding streams, and government oversight, were never designed to be agile, innovative, or flexible. We will continue to fail future generations unless we can reinvent our education institutions to meet the world as it evolves, not as we have all experienced it. The very real risk we face in the coming decades is a fundamental collapse of our established societal norms as we experience them today.

How Have We Tried to Address the Challenge to Improve Our Broken System?

Multiple well-intended attempts at major improvement have included experimental restructuring of failing schools; introducing a rigorous and more competitive curriculum with specialized testing; additional resources to help systems innovate; additional tests; and the continuation of alternative options such as magnet schools and charter schools. In the end, this traditional playbook for education gives *summative feedback or assessment*—a quiz at the end of the week or the semester, or a grade plopped meaninglessly into a pool of other grades that are often artificially inflated and not always connected to what was learned. That is, as well intentioned as the remedies have been, they have only addressed the symptoms of a bigger problem and not tackled the root cause, which is that the entire system needs a dramatic overhaul. Continuing in this way is like rearranging the deck chairs on the *Titanic* hoping for different results; inevitably, we will feel frustrated that we continue to falter as a nation.

CBE is an antidote to each of these concerns because it centers students, giving them agency and increasing their self-esteem. They no longer need to fear the measurement of their learning because they know where they are and where they're going, and they have multiple opportunities to show what they know and can do in a variety of ways.

Although some measurable improvements in student achievement have been documented, the vast majority of schools have fallen far short of deep transformation and, as a result, the COVID-19 pandemic has allowed our students' success rate to reach record lows (Kuhfeld, Soland, Lewis, & Morton, 2022).

What Has the Pandemic Revealed About the Broken Education System?

The COVID-19 pandemic has both exposed and underscored all our traditional educational shortcomings, as David Leonhardt (2022) illustrates brilliantly and viscerally in his *New York Times* article, "No Way to Grow Up." The crisis encompasses various aspects of students' well-being, including academic performance, mental health, and safety. Here are the key points that Leonhardt (2022) highlights.

- **Academic impact:** Students fell significantly behind in school during the first year of the pandemic. In the fall of the 2020–2021 school year, scores for mathematics and reading were lower than normal, with the greatest disparities in American Indian and Alaska Native, Black, Latino/a, and high-poverty communities (Lewis, Kuhfeld, Ruzek, & McEachin, 2021). Experts agree that it's an unprecedented academic achievement crisis.

- **Mental health challenges:** Students of all ages face mental health problems exacerbated by the pandemic. In 2021, several medical organizations declared a national state of emergency in young people's mental health, highlighting among other things a dramatic increase in emergency department visits for mental health emergencies, including suicide attempts (American Academy of Pediatrics, 2021). Suicide attempts increased, especially among adolescent girls; the rate of emergency department visits in the twelve- to seventeen-year-old age group increased by 51 percent from early 2019 to early 2021 (Yard et al., 2021).
- **Gun violence and crime:** Gun violence against children has increased, and school shooting incidents, after a drop in 2020, rose markedly the following year. They have continued to increase, with 82 incidents reported in 2023 (Matthews, 2023).
- **Disruptions in school life:** Many schools have not returned to normal, as staffing issues and burnout continue to impact things like lunchtimes, extracurricular activities, assemblies, school trips, parent-teacher conferences, and bus schedules. All these continue to contribute to learning loss and social isolation.
- **Behavioral issues:** Schools across the United States report upticks in disruptive behaviors, including obvious ones like vandalism or fighting and more subtle ones like refusing to participate in class (Belsha, 2021).
- **COVID variants:** Further variants of the virus, including Omicron and its subvariants, continue to cause disruptions as outbreaks lead to cancellations of sporting events and other activities and even temporary closings of whole districts (Goldstein, 2022).

The overall picture painted by the pandemic is one of a multifaceted crisis affecting the holistic well-being of U.S. students, with potential long-term consequences. Addressing these challenges will require coordinated efforts from educators, health care professionals, policymakers, and communities. This is why now is the time to overhaul our system.

Richard has spoken at length with hundreds of superintendents across the United States who admit their students are falling dramatically behind, both academically and socially. Lacking options, resources, and resilience, many schools were already treading water prepandemic and barely surviving day to day. Our system was not prepared and has not reacted quickly enough to handle this disruptive societal tsunami. The response to the worldwide health emergency failed to meet our instructional goals and was due in part to the current system. Student success is highly dependent on teacher-facilitated learning only. Students who were forced to work independently during the pandemic simply did not know how to be self-sufficient learners; meanwhile, in our observations, students in CBE systems handled the changes more smoothly because they are used to self-direction in their learning. The struggles of traditional schools are the fault not of our students or our teachers but rather of the system; nevertheless, it will take years to catch up and fill the learning gaps in many students' levels of competence.

"The coronavirus caused by far the biggest disruption in the history of American education," Meira Levinson and Daniel Markovits (2022) assert, describing the reality of the impact of COVID-19 in public schools. Alec MacGillis (2023) for ProPublica highlights the steep toll exacted on students, especially students of marginalized backgrounds. *New York Times* columnist David Brooks (2023) highlights the fallout: "Things have not reverted back to normal as COVID has gradually lost its grip on American life. Today's teachers and students are living with a set of altered realities, and they may be for the rest of their lives." Brooks (2023) goes on to list what these altered realities include.

- According to *Education Week*, U.S. public schools have lost over a million students (Dee, 2022).
- Those students who remain are struggling. NAEP results reveal that fourth and eighth graders have lost two decades' worth of progress (NCES, n.d.a, n.d.b); that means that in 2022, they were performing similarly to how they performed in the 1990s (Mervosh, 2022; Sparks, 2022).
- Schools are seeing a huge rise in chronic absenteeism, which means students are more likely to be disconnected from school and experiencing interrupted instruction (Jacobson, 2022).
- Students' behavior and social-emotional development have likewise worsened, according to NCES (2022) data, with more than 80 percent of public schools reporting that the pandemic and its lingering effects have had a negative impact.

This significant disruption in education precipitated by the pandemic has exacerbated and exposed the fundamental failures of our present education system but may also have created the perfect storm to reflect and reinvent what we want our schools to be like in the future. This should be a call to action not only for the United States but for every nation to assess and rethink how the world can best educate all students to find personal success and fulfillment in their future. We cannot allow an inferior system to dictate the future of our nation's potential. This failed system will continue to force a future generation of young learners to educate themselves outside of the classroom and be tested daily on what matters most in the world they were born into. We must design and implement a new system by ridding ourselves of rigid, baked-in, and misguided classroom protocols, political policy mistakes, and a host of other district-by-district, community-driven prejudices and misconceptions working against improving our students' futures.

This is not a new narrative for our country's often failing education system, but it has rekindled the spark of a long overdue revolution around substantial school reform because of the disruption that occurred with the virus. Due to the disruptive change in work habits and career goals, both teacher and administration attrition rate is at an all-time high (American University School of Education, 2021; Barnum, 2023; Diliberti & Schwartz, 2023). The serendipity of the scale of turnover with veteran education professionals may be that we have a once-in-a-decade opportunity to use this watershed moment to build a delivery system of life-skill development suited for the next generation of educators and students.

What Are the Takeaways From This Chapter?

We believe that change in schools happens for two reasons. Either a situational crisis presents an unplanned opportunity where true leaders seize the moment and take advantage of the urgency to adjust the norms, or a burning platform presents itself and cannot be ignored, such as the global pandemic or the many fallow years prior to the pandemic with rapidly escalating poor student achievement results. Of the two, the latter has the most explosive leverage to make the impossible possible. Finland's education system is a classic example. When the country departed from the Soviet Union, Finland's leaders recognized their economic future rested heavily on the quality of their education system. The new nation quickly made education the top priority and infused the latest research about learning into its schools. Finland set out to create the best traditional schools using the latest in materials and teaching techniques and then carefully measured its results (OECD, 2010). In the latest worldwide PISA, in which the United States achieves a middling ranking, Finland's results score at or near the top in every category (OECD, 2019). Along with other high-performing nations like China and Singapore, it has carefully maximized the potential of a traditional time-based system.

Could our nation ever reach the levels of success with a traditional time-based classroom model that Finland has enjoyed? Finland took advantage of an opportunity to reinvent its education system when it left the Soviet Union, and the United States now faces a similar opportunity after the pandemic. While the crisis has always been there, the pandemic poured fuel on the fire of the burning platform. But the time-based model is not the best way to go about this reinvention. For real postpandemic change, CBE is the answer.

Even as well as Finland's educational system may seem to be functioning, the future holds steep challenges for the static delivery model, which, in the eyes of Finland's students, ignores and marginalizes the effects of global-based social media and the technological advancements in all areas of the economy, including AI (European Commission, 2021). Students, as citizens of the new world, will surely demand change and create a tectonic shift in the norms. Conflict is inevitable.

We need to improve beyond the limits of traditional schools and design learning ecosystems of the future created around best practices linked to our nation's shared beliefs. The United States needs to move toward core beliefs and actions that focus on recognizing that all students are unique and desperately need a better approach to learning for their future job opportunities. When we collectively recognize that our schools are failing and commit ourselves to creating something better, only then will we shoulder the challenge to better meet the future needs of every student.

We must search for those classrooms, schools, and districts that already exist with a solid platform of these forward-reaching characteristics. What can we learn from the best models out there? What impact have they had on students' success in improving learning beyond a traditional classroom? Did these new systems prepare their students to be better able to navigate their own journey in life? If these models don't exist, how do we go about creating the conditions to allow these types of learning ecosystems to begin? If we can successfully create them, can we then replicate and scale them up to a national movement?

These next series of educational reforms will be the greatest pivotal moment not only for our present students, but for the future of society as we know it. This may be our last chance to reset the algorithm of learning, and this book was written to give guidance and clarity on how to proceed. Whether you are a teacher, principal, superintendent, parent, or student, we all have a role to play. Even if only one educator makes the effort to bring this vision forward from this blueprint, this book will have been worth the effort. The next chapter discusses the promise of CBE to address the problems we've highlighted.

CHAPTER 2

A Revolutionary Future for Learning

Change is never easy, and our educational institutions will defend the status quo even if we know it doesn't work, because it is all we know. But as we've demonstrated, change *is* possible.

Throughout history, there have been pivotal moments in humankind's development. These moments have been often riddled with suspicion, ridicule, and even a touch of hopefulness. CBE is such a moment. Anytime you disrupt the routine of how things are done, there is often strong resistance; but soon afterward, a groundswell of support develops when people realize that this is a better way of helping all students. CBE is a different way of educating our students and, like other innovations, has been met with resistance if for no other reason than it's unfamiliar.

The essential questions this chapter covers include the following.

- What is CBE, and why is it the education model for the future?
- What are the key elements and benefits of CBE?
- What are the first critical steps before implementing a CBE system?
- How do leaders begin the process of implementing CBE?
- Where is CBE working?
- What are the takeaways from this chapter?

What Is CBE, and Why Is It the Education Model for the Future?

Competency-based education (sometimes called proficiency- or mastery-based education) puts students at the center of their learning. Schools help guide them to find their pathway in life. The big difference from traditional schooling is that CBE promotes mastery of content and not simply covering the material. This sets in motion a new way of teaching, learning, grading, reporting, and supporting students unlike anything we have seen in the past. The change is deep and often requires entire schools to create, implement, and evaluate something entirely new. This methodology prepares students for their future in a way current schools fail to do. The challenge is fourfold to scale this vision. First, how can districts establish a proof of concept within an entire K–12 system that adheres to a quality CBE philosophy to see that it can work with students from their schools? Second, how can districts ensure sustainability over years of leadership and school board attrition? Third, can CBE be sustained and replicated in a variety of schools and districts that represent the entire country? Fourth, can CBE be scaled to radically alter the education landscape, thus becoming a better way of helping our students find success?

Educators and policymakers must work together to place student success at the center of any discussion concerning improvement and instructional reform. This student-centered focus should be non-negotiable. If we want to be serious about providing a better experience in our schools, we must first commit our collective will to demand that our mission includes meeting all students where they are on their personal learning journey and taking them onward to their next step toward a lifetime of accomplishment and success.

Since the 1990s, schools have responded to society's criticism with a confetti of ambitious mission and vision statements mentioning these exact observations and sentiments, but rarely do our institutions establish any metrics, strategies, or outcomes to measure their success in reaching these important objectives. Simply visit any school, and you will see a mission and vison statement colorfully postered, but when you ask anyone how they measure their progress, the conversation quickly changes. If you do find a school that can provide metrics to support their vision, often it's only an afterthought, and there is no trend data from year to year. Business leaders and public policymakers have generated commonsense recommendations on the critical skills and dispositions students need to meet the changing nature of our nation's workforce. We need to walk the talk if our primary goal is to achieve better over-the-horizon outcomes for our students. Our journey begins with a set of beliefs and values around learning that is supported by all stakeholders (see figure 2.1). These beliefs must be the foundational building blocks of how we educate and prepare our students to be happy and productive adults. We want our next generation to be constantly on a path of lifelong learning, self-exploration, and personal growth.

Once there is an established a set of agreed-on beliefs in a school community, the next step is to envision how this revolutionary structure for each student's learning paradigm would look in practical terms. This brave-new-world school would shuffle the key puzzle pieces of content management, instructional delivery, scheduling, grading, grouping and ungrouping students, assessment tools, report cards, honor

CBE Values and Beliefs Around Learning	
1	Every student needs to learn in an environment that is safe, dynamic, and supportive.
2	Every student is unique; individual students need to understand themselves and how they relate to and interact productively in a learning environment with both peers and adults.
3	Learning is about developing the wellness of each student including the academic, physical, and emotional dimensions of a student.
4	Every student learns in a different way and at a different rate. All students are special learners and have unique learning styles.
5	Learning needs to be transparent so that it can happen anywhere, anyplace, and anytime.
6	Every student needs to be deeply engaged in their educational plan and understand the purpose and progression of the concepts and content of what they are learning.
7	Learning needs to be future focused, embracing technology, global thinking, and evolving innovations.
8	Learning needs to allow students to accelerate their own path, both in the amount of content and in the depth of understanding.
9	A student-led, teacher-assisted commitment to demonstrated mastery of content versus rewarding collective time spent in covering the material is a crucial factor in CBE and supports a growth-based and self-disciplined mindset, minimizing opportunity for failure within the system.
10	Every student should be in personal control of their learning plan to create ambitious goals, to maximize their own potential, and to make a meaningful contribution to mankind.

Figure 2.1: CBE educational reform values and beliefs.

roll, graduation requirements, and, finally, a seamless university or workforce transition. Many schools have made attempts to reimagine the stacking of some of these desired elements, but few have made the quantum leap involving all these elements at once. Dynamics of the classroom for all students begin to transform by moving away from seat time and high-stakes testing and replacing it with mastery gained through teacher-assisted exploration, best described as competency-based education.

This critical systemic shift is the pivotal point that will affect everything else we do and, when deployed with increasing fidelity, will have a seismic impact on our current system.

What Are the Key Elements and Benefits of CBE?

CBE begins by defining what skills students need to acquire to become successful in the future, followed by determining how each student learns best and creating a meaningful pathway that will engage each learner in their personal quest to master a problem or demonstrate understanding of a new concept. CBE helps everyone involved in this critical process to be on the same page in terms of teaching and learning. In visiting hundreds of classrooms over the years, we find that in the traditional or time-based schools, there is little consistency in successful outcomes from class to class, grade to grade, or school to school. Teachers often struggle to find the best practices in isolation, resulting in a very checkered story of success with an inefficient, confusing system.

Observing two same-grade classes within the same school and encountering completely different teacher-to-student delivery strategies and resulting learning outcomes is a common occurrence. Everything from what and how teachers teach, to how schools assess and report their students' achievement, to strategies for improving the student experience both inside and outside of the classroom lacks any systematic approach to addressing real-life challenges. There is certainly scant evidence of a guaranteed success rate for all students even in many of our highest-performing school systems. These achievement results raise important questions.

- Are we as stakeholders really still declaring that a D grade is an acceptable outcome in any learning module preparing students for the future?
- Would anyone want their doctor, pilot, or tax attorney to have achieved barely passing grades with less-than-average proficiency on a measurement of mastery in their professional field of study?

A well-deployed CBE model eliminates the burdensome task of subjective grading along with a report card's narrow vision and inconsistent nature of assessment. This proven approach to learning aligns the high-performance values and beliefs around best practices of instruction and delivers learning in a more effective and creative way. Teachers provide the pathway and certify competency after embracing a continuous feedback loop based on formative data and student performance. Research shows clearly that this student-driven model touches on all the critical components of an effective district-level learning system (Sudderth, n.d.). CBE in isolated classrooms is successful but will not get our nation's schools to world-class results. CBE is a powerful learning approach that takes advantage of the latest technology and research to focus on the potential for success for every student based on how, why, and when learning happens. Building a culture of success for every student unleashes teachers to take failure out of the equation and create a positive classroom environment. CBE expands the world of learning possibilities off campus and into the larger community, where students pursue authentic tasks.

The key elements and benefits of a CBE system compared to a traditional system of education positively impact all aspects of the student and educator experience. With instruction, for example, in a traditional system, teachers provide information that the majority of the students in the middle ground of comprehension can engage with. Everyone goes at the same pace, since the teacher can only manage to instruct with the whole group together. In the CBE system, students receive instruction at their level at the pace with which they can succeed—whether it is faster, slower, or the same as others. This is possible—and manageable—because CBE ensures processes are in place to support it: that is, differentiated resources, student ownership of the environment where they are learning so they know what to do, and a digital platform to assist students with their individual needs as the teacher makes rounds for the hands-on activities happening in the classroom. Much of the instruction may be multidisciplinary, bridging lessons from mathematics and science with language arts, culture, history, and personal social skills. The benefits of the CBE system are that students learn beyond just a skills level, apply what they learn so it goes deeper, and build on it. Figure 2.2 provides a summary.

Instruction

Traditional System

One-size-fits-all textbook sets the pace. Students move on even if they are not ready for next steps. Whole-group instruction is predominant.

Application of skills is minimal.

Prescribed programs and textbooks drive instruction.

CBE System

Instruction is balanced (students must understand the information and apply it in real-life situations whenever possible).

Instruction is differentiated, thus meeting individual students at the point of their need and interest.

Textbooks are still valued, but learning outcomes or competencies drive the instruction.

Benefits

Needs of all students are met not only to meet one year's growth in one year's time but to increase the rate of learning for all students.

Instruction is not just about learning the skills but about applying the skills in a meaningful way, thereby increasing student engagement. Emphasis is on real-world problems in a safe environment.

Example

Students begin where they need instruction and move forward from that point with the pace based on their learning. Instruction is personalized and relevant.

Figure 2.2: Elements and benefits of a CBE system—Instruction.

CBE benefits also extend, as discussed, into students' agency—their voice and choice. As figure 2.3 shows, in traditional systems, students' voice and choice are rare. It takes an outstanding teacher, who can manage the classroom in a way that builds trust with students, to allow them to be part of the decision-making process. Teachers in a CBE system must be open to the fact that they can learn from students. Before that trust is built, teachers can begin to allow choice through a variety of pathways to mastering the material, from *playlists*, or menus of resources for students to choose from, to individual and group projects that are monitored by the teacher to ensure quality. The classroom becomes a union of hearts and minds working together to discover learning in real ways. The benefit is deeper learning with students who are engaged and excited about learning.

Teachers and students in traditional systems can fall into a mentality where students play the game to guess what they need to do to pass. Traditional monitoring

Student Engagement (Voice and Choice)

Traditional System

Students are passive learners and are rarely engaged. Students cannot navigate their own learning.

CBE System

Because of the transparency of the learning targets, learning expectations are clear. Students take more ownership in their role as learners; therefore, they are more engaged and navigate their own learning.

Benefits

CBE increases student engagement and ownership. It also prepares students for the global economy by accelerating their learning, especially with 21st century skills.

Example

Students are partners in their learning. They have choices based on their interests within boundaries of necessary learning. They can see what is required and why and how to move forward to their next step.

Figure 2.3: Elements and benefits of a CBE system—Student engagement; voice and choice.

allows for a minimum amount of work to just pass to the next grade. In the CBE system, students monitor their own progress, receiving the help they need in areas they have not mastered and being allowed to move forward from the lessons they already know. The benefits include the knowledge that the students have of the process to make a difference in their own learning (see figure 2.4).

Grading is another area in which CBE differs widely from traditional systems. In traditional systems, students generally receive a grade from A to F, and everyone knows that a D is still passing, as long as students meet the minimum requirements. Grading often includes teacher impressions of effort and attitude, so students may pass even though they haven't really learned anything. Figure 2.5 (page 24) summarizes how, within the CBE system, students are able to see what educators expect before they begin; they also know that they must show mastery in a variety of ways before they move on. Also, once students have shown mastery, their scores are recorded in real time (not waiting for quarters or semesters) so they can monitor their own progress.

Monitoring Progress

Traditional System

Students move to the next grade level regardless of whether they have acquired the necessary skills.

CBE System

Students must achieve proficiency (or 80 percent and higher) to move to the next instructional level. Students are set up for success.

Benefits

Students are guaranteed prerequisite knowledge to be successful in their learning progression.

Due to the students' ownership, they are able to navigate their own progression.

Example

Students are able to see what is required to show mastery and know how to navigate their resources. They are part of a system that supports what they know and what they have learned.

Figure 2.4: Elements and benefits of a CBE system—Monitoring progress.

Grading

Traditional System	CBE System
A–F scoring based on arbitrary criteria. Example: Final quarter grades may be based on various combinations of participation, attendance, and test scores. • Attendance, 10 percent of grade • Homework, 25 percent • Behavior, 15 percent • Test scores, 50 percent	Grading is based on mastering individual standards. "A, B, or try again" scoring. Students have multiple opportunities to achieve and improve their grades. A minimum GPA for graduation is 3.0.
Benefits	**Example**
CBE creates transparent and consistent expectations across classrooms and sites so that students, parents, teachers, and administrators know what is expected at each stage of learning and the rigor to achieve mastery is not a moving target.	There is no guessing for what is required and why it is important. Grades are posted in real time and include in-depth projects and reflection on learning.

Figure 2.5: Elements and benefits of a CBE system—Grading.

Assessments in traditional systems are generally based on tests. These tests allow teachers the ability to see where students are in a moment of time of their learning. The CBE system uses tests, but they are just one of many types of assessments. Rubrics (or proficiency scales) are used from the start, so everyone—students, parents, and teachers—is clear about what is expected before instruction begins. Assessments are meant to show that students have mastered the standard in a variety of ways. This can be done whenever students feel they are ready. Ideally, students will see immediate results so they can go back and learn the parts that they might have missed and still need to learn. Students in the CBE system quickly realize that assessments are a great tool to help them see gaps and focus just on what they need—rather than a milestone to dread. Figure 2.6 provides a summary.

Collaboration is another area on which CBE hinges. Collaboration can be hit or miss in traditional systems; teachers often collaborate for thematic units or generally,

Assessments and Rubrics

Traditional System	CBE System
Teachers score students based on tests, attendance, and behavior. There is little consistency from class to class and subject to subject in grading and scoring. Assessments are primarily pencil-and-paper tests. Rigor rarely goes beyond skills-based recall. There is often very little correlation to state standards. Instruction is mostly textbook driven.	Assessments, tasks, and rubrics are tied directly to individual targets. Each target receives its own, separate score. Assessments go beyond pencil-and-paper tests and might include projects, presentations, collaboration between schools in different countries, and individual learning plans. Rigor is directly addressed in each rubric.
Benefits	**Example**
In CBE, the transparency of assessments is such that a student knows exactly what is required to pass each individual standard. Assessments and rubrics inherently allow for meaningful engagement and deeper rigor through the taxonomy and are agreed on and made in collaboration between student and teacher.	There are a variety of paths toward demonstrating mastery of learning. Students are able to choose from a variety of methods for proof of learning.

Figure 2.6: Elements and benefits of a CBE system—Assessments and rubrics.

especially in the elementary grades. But when teachers collaborate more intentionally, as they do in a CBE system (see figure 2.7, page 26), students are the ones who benefit the most, with common discussions happening on behalf of each student to ensure they get the experience they need to master their learning. With collaboration, teachers are allowed more creativity and ideas as they work together, rather than in isolation behind closed doors. Students benefit when they see their role models (the teachers) able to use their differences as strengths for teaching in a variety of ways and putting aside any disagreements for the greater good.

We also emphasize psychological safety above all else. When students and teachers feel safe, the environment is one of support and helpfulness. It's OK for both students

Collaboration

Traditional System	CBE System
Little to no formal collaboration among students or teachers. Each student is responsible for their work only.	CBE helps create a safe environment to not only learn from failures but embrace working together with others who might not share common skills.

Benefits	Example
In CBE, collaboration among peers demonstrates a safe environment where risk in allowed and failure is used as a learning tool.	Collaboration among staff members provides role models for students to collaborate on projects. Students see the benefit of combining a variety of talents and experiences to explore topics and have time to be curious.

Figure 2.7: Elements and benefits of a CBE system—Collaboration.

and teachers to make mistakes, knowing that no one will laugh at you or bully you, whether it's a fellow student or a colleague. Students begin to own their space, and the learning environment becomes a community (see figure 2.8).

One final element we must note is a comprehensive CBE digital platform that helps deploy and monitor every aspect of this paradigm shift. Districts have to either build on their existing learning management system (LMS) or adopt a completely new platform that can help manage the student, teacher, and systems data. The challenge with traditional learning management systems is that they are not designed to support a CBE system. They measure students' progress based on traditional content and grading and are unable to measure specific learning objectives, which is at the heart of CBE. See figure 2.9 for a comparison between a traditional LMS and a CBE digital platform. A platform designed to support CBE is critical to scale the vision. Besides managing student progress, the program needs to manage and provide real-time data on teachers and administrators, monitoring their competencies in the change process.

The CBE platform provides clear dashboards and contains "evergreen" data, updated in real time, so adjustments can continue to be made in the timely rollout of this

Safety

Traditional System

Strict rules are enforced to ensure everyone follows the guidelines.

CBE System

Codes of conduct are created together with students and teachers facilitating, so students feel a sense of ownership and pride in their environment.

Benefits

Safety is considered a responsibility that all share. With a safe environment, discipline issues decrease.

Example

Establishing a code of collaboration gives the students a visual reminder of what they agreed to support for everyone's learning environment.

Figure 2.8: Elements and benefits of a CBE system—Safety.

LMS Comparison

Traditional LMS	CBE LMS
Designed for adult convenience	Designed to be learner centered
Focuses on content	Focuses on learning and growth
Time-based progression	Mastery-based progression
Built around traditional A, B, C grading system	Built around competencies and rubrics
Linear and predetermined learning	Personalized learning based on learner needs and interests
Focuses on course completion	Focuses on skill mastery
Time-based learning	Anytime, anywhere learning

Figure 2.9: Comparing traditional and CBE LMS platforms.

system. It is possible to do this in a classroom without the platform beginning with the flipped classroom and then moving toward mastery learning, but to scale efficiently you will need a robust digital platform. In 1994, when Richard's district built the first platform, they used FileMaker Pro—an indication of how much technology has changed. Now we have new advances in technology, especially with the introduction of AI, which makes this vision for all students scalable even in the largest school system or country. When applying this strategy during his work in Russia, Richard began with developing the digital platform and then hiring teams of content professionals to develop engaging content so students would constantly be embracing an expanding experience of self-discovery. The acceleration of AI for educational reform has made the transition to CBE even more important, explosive, and challenging.

The change commitment begins when teachers volunteer to learn how to shift their traditional classrooms into competency-based ones to demonstrate how this globally proven concept will work with all our students. Teachers need to be trained on every level of this new system, beginning with how to create a collaborative culture and including learning to use the tools and processes to gradually release control for learning directly to the students. Finally, there is a moment when the culture of the classrooms is transformed to help all students learn individually in an accelerated manner. We like to say it's a magical moment, but the magic is really in the hard work of the students, teachers, and leaders who have brought it about. Initially, in the journey of any educational institution, teachers begin to slowly shift the culture of the classroom and the school to the new paradigm. This creates what we call a *proof of concept.* The task then becomes how to link the subject content to the engine of change and unleash the power of CBE for all students.

What Are the First Critical Steps Before Implementing a CBE System?

Pursuing substantive change to address this monumental breakdown in our education system can be like navigating a minefield, derailing the CBE mission for change before results are realized. At every challenging level of moving toward better outcomes for all students, multiple pitfalls can easily discourage participants from continuing with this uphill battle for the future of our schools.

Several puzzle pieces need to be considered present or at least within possibility before beginning this important journey toward student success. Does your present education community display the following seven attributes?

1. A belief that hard facts and proven gold-star results will create a desire by key leaders to see the value, importance, and benefits that a commitment to CBE offers
2. An overall desire to create a positive culture and mission in your school or district that is committed to embracing the CBE approach

3. District- and school-level systems for collaboration, including district and school leadership teams (DLTs and SLTs) and professional learning communities (PLCs), acting to unify a shared commitment to ensure all students achieve success
4. Familiarity with second-order change, which requires a different skill set for your leadership team than it may be used to
5. Recognition that CBE requires a continual and sustained effort with many peaks and valleys and that professional responsibilities will change over time
6. Communication, honesty, and transparency, which are vital to sustain this revolution
7. A commitment to help others on their CBE journey by opening your classrooms and schools to other educators

Leadership is by far the most critical ingredient that will determine success as a system (see chapters 5, page 113, and 6, page 139). We find you need both a bottom-up approach (from the classroom level) and a top-down approach (leadership), beginning with the commitment to the values and beliefs driving this need for change.

The local top-down approach means the administrative leader needs to believe and commit to this journey by actively participating in or, ideally, leading the change. Initially, a new type of leader may be necessary, one who goes beyond being a competent manager and becomes a change agent who inspires others to join in this journey. Initially, CBE leaders need a new set of playbooks that go far beyond being a competent manager. True leaders must dare to become ferocious agents of change. A leader with all the right tools and community support is able to guide this journey and build synergy, a shared vision, and a culture for success. The bottom-up approach is where empowered teachers volunteer to learn how to shift their traditional classrooms into competency-based ones to demonstrate to naysayers that this, in fact, will work with all our students. The challenge, once student success is demonstrated at a local level, is to scale up this program's promise to a tsunami of committed student-centered schools involved in revolutionary CBE.

If you are leading a larger school district of over fifty thousand students, the change factor becomes much more complex. The logistics of retooling years of sit-and-get classroom activity become much more of a challenge when retraining thousands of veteran educators at one time.

If such potential for change is not possible at your district level but you have schools interested in moving toward the future, a clearly defined process needs to be developed to allow willing schools and master teachers an adequate span of time to innovate change and get their feet wet in CBE. The challenge with this approach is that they will be running a dual system under a microscope until the entire district commits to instructional change.

Even though the CBE system has tremendous potential in improving student outcomes, the challenge is how to move glacier-like institutions into this new reality, especially since very few schools have experienced this new paradigm and can clearly demonstrate its value. You can't simply impose this new system from the top down onto the backs of your educators and expect them all to flourish. This change process often begins with an initial conversation or dialogue with key policy leaders and quickly expands out to all stakeholders. First, you need to begin by asking difficult questions around the readiness of your targeted schools and facilitate deep conversations with all stakeholders involved, including students, to explore and understand what could be possible in the near future.

To begin a discussion around CBE, we recommend these four communitywide questions.

1. What do our current data on student achievement, emotional wellness, student attrition, and in-school safety tell us about our programs and students?
2. What cadre of skills will our students need to be successful now and in the future?
3. What does our district's research and resource investment planning reveal about the most successful schools in our district and those schools that are underperforming in meeting all students' needs?
4. What are the changes to the beliefs and values our schools cherish? How can we find common ground to change the present community vision around measuring and striving toward success for some, but not all, of our students and guarantee our schools will better prepare our students for their future?

The question of targeting and evaluating the success of classrooms and larger cohorts of CBE-minded educators and their success begins with effective and timely certification of student competencies that can turn the tide on failure. The national statistics will improve if teachers have the power to target student learning differences and prescribe strategies to always move forward toward a learning goal without anxiety and stressful, time-dictated measurements that are presently only working for a very few students and leaving the rest of the class struggling and defeated in meeting arbitrary deadlines for attaining a passing grade.

What we have learned over several decades of guiding school change is that it is never linear and there will always be multiple issues to navigate. There are many ways to change any system, but in schools when it involves so many stakeholder groups, the complexity increases tenfold. We have found that there are critical steps that have proven successful in the United States and internationally (see figure 2.10).

	CBE Getting Started
	Conversation With Stakeholders Bring together all stakeholders and lead the conversation with essential questions to determine shared beliefs and the vision around learning.
	Provide Data on Education Provide stakeholders compelling data around student achievement, wellness, safety, and future opportunities.
	Create a Collaborative Culture Create a positive collaborative culture to support the collective vision.
	Set Priorities for Students' Learning Determine what students really need to know to be successful in life, and reverse engineer those desired learning traits from graduation to primary grades.
	Scope and Sequence Create a clear scope and sequence of learning targets, assessments, and reporting progress and adopt an instructional philosophy to engage students at multiple levels.
	Switch From Time-Based to Performance-Based Learning Make a commitment to shift away from time-based sit-and-get learning and toward a personal competency-based learning system that connects learning K–20.
	Continue to Innovate Continue to innovate and improve student happiness and mental health based on the data and feedback from all off-campus and in-house stakeholders.
	Let Technology Help You Get There Utilize technology and evergreen data to help guide and support all students and enhance their journey toward a healthy and successful life.

Figure 2.10: Getting started with CBE.

How Do Leaders Begin the Process of Implementing CBE?

Whenever possible, our solution is to promote a systemwide, systematic approach to CBE—primarily because it will be sustainable even after the attrition of current leaders. Our goal is to share with you the very best of what we have learned thus far in our journey. There are many components that make up an effective CBE system. It is important that educators have a strong grasp of the importance of each component. But more importantly, they need to be willing to change and adapt new components if they are not getting necessary results. Often when attempting any kind of change, there needs to be a clear understanding not only of why we are committed but of how we implement change with fidelity. Even when schools are committed to moving toward this new system, we often see bits and pieces of CBE, thereby limiting the full impact of this philosophy. Cherry-picking a few of the components of CBE won't accomplish the full spectrum.

Leaders sometimes share that they have fully embraced CBE because they have adopted new policies, changed report cards, created new schedules, and so on, but when we check for full deployment in the classrooms, only a fraction of the teachers actually have embraced the change.

For example, when administering feedback reports to schools and districts, there is often a gap between the perceived implementation and the real implementation of CBE. Just because there is a robust digital platform loaded with content and everyone has been trained doesn't mean it is being deployed by all. Often only a small percentage of educators are actually using the platform on a regular basis. Our goal is to give you a clear road map of the critical elements of CBE and a sequence of when and how to implement them to ensure fidelity and sustainability.

We have created a tool that helps individuals and organizations frame their journey. The six CBE progression stages are not necessarily a linear process; this tool (see figure 2.11) is designed to help stakeholders track their progress on the journey. The following chapters provide much more detail about how this process unfolds at the classroom, school, and district levels.

If you are a committed state or national leader and support this type of change, this is a perfect opportunity to create a seamless K–20 organization that potentially could alter the future for every student in a positive way by allowing acceleration and motivation to encourage those students willing and able to progress quickly through our antiquated, bureaucratic, and expensive system.

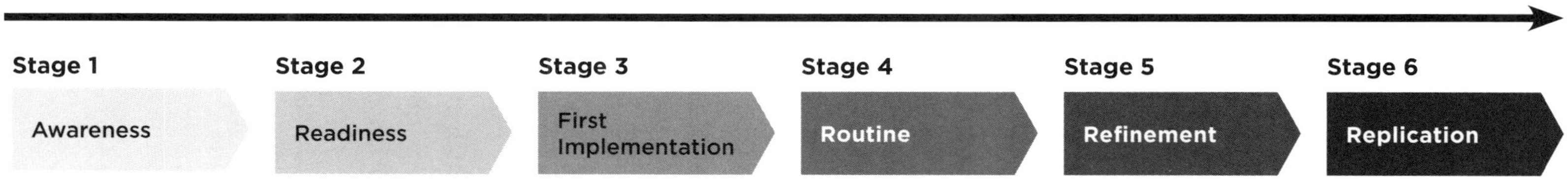

Stage 1	Awareness	You have pledged to learn more about this new approach to learning and have begun to build your district's capacity to commit to it.
Stage 2	Readiness	You have self-assessed using a CBE readiness survey and understand the key components in the road map.
Stage 3	First Implementation	You have committed and begun the journey by creating a timeline on your CBE road map. You have involved all your stakeholder groups in embracing this journey by creating a shared vision and code of collaboration.
Stage 4	Routine	All your educators have committed, and you have made progress in each area of your road map.
Stage 5	Refinement	You are now refining your processes based on data and have made several progressions.
Stage 6	Replication	You have reached the refinement stage in each area, you have years of positive data, and you are willing to help others in their journey.

Figure 2.11: Six progression stages of CBE.

Alongside implementation, we also recommend the following.

1. Develop a comprehensive waiver system for five years to free up districts to deploy this new system within a renewal process transparent to all stakeholders.
2. Create bipartisan support within the school community so everyone has an equal footing and opportunity to participate.
3. Provide necessary training and support for those schools committed to change.
4. Provide the heavy lifting support necessary, which includes selecting or creating a digital platform that contains the learning targets or outcomes, assessments, and reporting tools while providing real-time data.
5. Change or modify local policies and advocate to change national policies to support this innovation (transcripts, college admittance, eligibility, teacher certification, and so on).

Where Is CBE Working?

Delivering on the Promise: The Education Revolution (DeLorenzo, Battino, Schreiber, & Gaddy Carrio, 2008) gives a detailed account of the journey of Chugach School District in Alaska, where Richard, as superintendent, implemented CBE. As a result of the success there, interest in our work continued to grow and underscore the value of CBE. David Broder (2002), a syndicated columnist for *The Washington Post*, wrote a Sunday editorial applauding the tenets of competency-based teaching and the remarkable story of Chugach, which won the Malcolm Baldrige National Quality Award and launched our work onto the global stage.

Soon after receiving the Malcom Baldridge award, Richard founded the Re-Inventing Schools Coalition (RISC) in 2002 with the lofty mission to impact schools worldwide. Since then, Richard has successfully transformed thousands of schools throughout the United States and elsewhere, most notably in the Westminster Public Schools district just north of Denver, Colorado (www.westminsterpublicschools.org), and in the Lindsay Unified School District (2017) near Fresno, California (www.lindsay.k12.ca.us).

Because of its nature, CBE is challenging to measure, and researchers have had some difficulty isolating CBE initiatives enough to get a sense of their impact;

however, educators in CBE systems feel strongly that this system improves achievement and reduces equity gaps (Evans, Landl, & Thompson, 2021; Rix, 2023). Lindsay Unified School District began in 1990 to identify the barriers that it needed to overcome, including gangs, dropout rates, drugs, unemployment, poverty, language barriers, teenage pregnancy, and poor academic performance (Lindsay Unified, 2023). In 2005, Lindsay started addressing culture, first with Bea McGarvey, and in 2006, Chuck Schwan joined the movement to transform the district from a time-bound to a mastery-based system that was learner centered. In 2007, the district collaborated with the community by asking five questions (Lindsay Unified, 2023).

1. Why do we exist?
2. What values will govern how we interact with each other?
3. What is our ideal future?
4. What is the description of our graduate?
5. What are the principles around which we make decisions?

Through those collaborative discussions, Lindsay created consensus around five basic concepts: (1) shared vision, (2) core values, (3) vision statements, (4) lifelong learning standards, and (5) guided principles. They created a common language, the most important of which was that students became known as *learners* and teachers became known as *learning facilitators*. Starting with K–6, Lindsay expanded implementation to all grades through twelfth by 2011. After two years of checking and adjusting, Lindsay adopted a full performance-based system (Lindsay Unified, 2023). Learners published a book with their stories of success and challenges titled *Among the Groves: Lindsay Lives* by Jyothi Bathina (2011).

Lindsay, which serves a primarily Latino/a student population, won a prestigious award for its innovation and success in weathering the COVID-19 pandemic (Obeng, 2020). Its competency-based digital platform, Empower, helped Lindsay students and teachers stay focused on fulfilling their education goals (Obeng, 2020; Sommer, 2020). Lindsay identifies its core values, equity foundation, and personalized supports as the major keys to its ability to overcome pandemic-related challenges (Sommer, 2020).

The Proving Ground for Change

Following my years in the classroom, I became a school administrator in the Chugach School District in Alaska. I inherited a challenging burning platform in terms of both poor student academic achievement and a high potential for a lack of student success in the workforce after graduation. Ninety percent of our students could not read at grade level, and our graduates simply were not prepared for life in the world or in their local community after graduation. Real data were rarely presented to parents, and there seemed to be this universal acceptance that things were always just good enough. There existed a blind trust that schools know best and will do the job if parents and policymakers just accept the misguided premise that things will always be more beneficial for students without the turmoil and conflict of radical change. It was easier for parents, educators, and administration to go along and get along in this isolated Alaskan Native community. The school was failing daily in its promise on multiple levels that had been the status quo for many decades.

I committed myself to finding a way to help the students under my watch to break this mold and strive toward a new vision for the role the school could play in their community. We were transparent with our recent testing results and presented openly the real-time data about the village's students' performance, and both parents and staff members were surprised and alarmed. Once we shared the painful reality of the current testing results, our leadership team decided to invite all our stakeholders to join a novel visioning process to help us decide the future directions our schools could take to improve results. Most of my teachers at first seemed to be uneasy about this process since we were the experts, and asking our community for their reaction to bad news and soliciting collective input on solutions could only open a Pandora's box of uncertainties. It is always extremely difficult to even ask the question when those who are trusted to be in charge don't know all the answers. This common conundrum is where leadership needs to have the skills and tools necessary to carefully guide this process in ways that value all opinions, ideas, and strategies so the end results are a clear win-win for everyone. This process in Chugach began with uncovering the right questions from the community and from the professional staff concerning both the challenges identified and opportunities available to draw upon.

My research and my passion to push toward success on behalf of Chugach students who faced learning hurdles unimaginable to their peers in classrooms across our country led me to a bold plan to push aside the restrictions of the assembly-line American education system that was envisioned by Horace Mann and proven in the business world by Henry Ford (Williams, 2023). My background in special education is based on the premise that everyone needs the opportunity and resources to meet their own personal plan designed specifically to reach their potential. Simply stated, all students are special. Putting each student at the center of a delivery and support system that is linked to measurable goals through continuous improvement that constantly searches for new and improved learning outcomes was our goal. Every aspect of measuring student deliverables and designing the next stage of personal development and success was on the table. We embraced a continuous improvement mindset and checked and adjusted our strategies at each stage along the way.

We retrained our staff and sought out like-minded professionals necessary for our team approach to each student to help us reach our shared goals. This was the genesis of the first K–12 CBE system in the United States. Parents, students, and policymakers embraced the concept that all students should receive the chance to grow and thrive on their own timeline and in their own way. Our job was to demand continuous improvement for all students and relentlessly monitor their growth and success. Our teachers slowly developed an efficient and effective menu of assessment strategies that kept us on track.

After showing tremendous achievement growth year after year, the concept gained traction in our state, but we wanted validation that we were doing everything possible to help improve our system. We also wanted to be able to replicate our approach elsewhere so it would be sustainable with the normal attrition of our current staff. Our fervent belief we were on the right track led to statewide opportunities to share the value of this effort. Student-led and supportive opportunities to share their personal growth experiences in achieving excellence were greeted by media and politicians with open arms. Our belief in CBE was proven effective, and we celebrated with each graduate of our system the enormous increase in the expanded opportunities available for their ongoing learning and exploration in life.

The most rigorous and competitive validation of performance and excellence is found in the business world. The Malcolm Baldrige National Quality Award, named after the former secretary of commerce during Reagan's administration, is now recognized as the pinnacle of the pyramid for innovation and sustainable growth. There was not yet an education pathway when we decided to commit to this journey to prove the value of our design for educational reform, so we translated many of the business criteria and verbiage into education language. There had never been an educational or instructional winner to date even though many had attempted the challenge. Since we had little chance of winning this award, our primary reason for applying was to receive a useful third-party feedback report that carefully analyzed every aspect of our organization so that we could continue to improve.

The Malcolm Baldrige award was a business milestone of the highest order given rarely by the president of the United States. Organizations must prove that they are world class in seven critical categories with sustainable, positive trending data over five years. Organizations spend decades trying to receive this prestigious validation. The application process was extensive and comprehensive, involving months of work from my very dedicated team. We gained value through this self-assessment process, and I recommend this strategy of continuous improvement to any organization reaching for the gold ring of superior performance and success.

Several months later, I received a call at 5:00 a.m. from a gentleman claiming to be Secretary of Commerce Don Evans to congratulate us as the first winners of the Malcolm Baldrige award for education. In my half-awake slumber, I dismissed this as a colleague playing a prank, and I hung up on the call. Later that morning, when I looked at the call's area code, it read Washington, DC. Surprisingly, it was in fact Secretary Evans, and I returned the call to learn we had been awarded the distinction for organization excellence in 2001. Saying I was sorry never felt so good.

—RICHARD A. DELORENZO

In Richard's conversations with many leaders about their reluctance to commit to this change, this is what they shared.

- They feel overwhelmed and time stressed by simply managing the current system during these challenging times.
- Their schools are good enough; why take the risk when most parents are satisfied?
- There is a lack of trust and confidence within the school district between different stakeholder groups.
- This is a multiyear commitment, and key leaders of change will be leaving in the near future.
- This will disrupt everything they do currently, and they don't have confidence in their skills to see it through to the future.
- They want to see actual districts like theirs that have been successful before considering this challenge.
- If this is so good, why aren't there many other districts doing this?

These are all very real concerns from active practitioners. One of our challenges to scale this vision is to first find existing courageous educators who recognize the limitations of our current system and are willing to commit to this arduous journey. What gives us hope is that the pandemic exposed the very real weakness in student retention that CBE would solve. Students in CBE schools do not regress in achievement scores as so often happens in traditional school settings (Haynes et al., 2016), and we observed this to be so even with the effects of the pandemic. Those students owned their learning accomplishments and had the skills baked into their learning style to continue to navigate their growth and progress through their grade levels. CBE students know how to learn and retain their competency through their ongoing stages of exploration.

Reflections From Introducing and Scaling CBE in Russia

Just before the global pandemic broke out, I had a unique opportunity to bring this vision to impact not just a large district or state, but an entire country. I was invited to bring a large team of talented and committed professionals to Russia, and with the support of a key political leader, I was able to scale up this vision and strategies to potentially impact millions of students. At the peak of this exciting work, we were training thousands of educators each week to rethink how learning can be more effective and more focused on individual student achievement.

While CBE training was underway in Russian schools, multiple dramatic changes were happening at once. On the spectrum for substantive change was everything from teacher training and evaluation methods for students to streamlining and modifying policies that only supported the traditional system (high-stakes assessments, grading, promoting students, grouping and ungrouping, eligibility, and so on). An entire education delivery system was in the process of being overhauled. Those of us leading the effort learned to negotiate in that sweet spot where truth, proven research, candor, and humor could find the key to common ground even when the debates became heated.

COVID-19 was the unimaginable and unplanned event that placed all the innovation and collective Russian commitment on hold. Then Russia's invasion of Ukraine disrupted all aspects of Russia's human infrastructure (to say nothing of its impact on the people of Ukraine) and the next chapter of this massive educational reform effort is currently scaled back.

This fledgling effort, which is currently in a holding pattern, will eventually be a successful experiment so long as national leaders who control the funding see the economic benefit of empowering and equipping through education the next generations of learners (DeLorenzo, 2020).

—RICHARD A. DELORENZO

What Are the Takeaways From This Chapter?

Although our first successes in helping other schools were profound and encouraging, we needed to find a better way to scale up this vision quickly if we were going to reach the tipping point of changing the landscape of American schools. The elements and benefits that we have described in this chapter are profound and compelling, but as we have also discussed, there are real challenges facing schools that want to implement CBE. Schools must take many steps before even beginning the process of implementation, which in itself is a complicated and many-faceted undertaking.

The promise of CBE has yet to reach the critical mass of impacting our entire national educational delivery system for many reasons. Primary among these is the hurdle of overcoming the inertia of the traditional system, which has been cemented in school culture, entrenched by policies enacted and designed to protect the lucrative testing industry that feeds on the present system. Even though many leaders agree with the promise of this program, very few step up and commit themselves to this type of radical upheaval. Change is never dull or easy, especially when it impacts an entire system. We believe we are at an inflection point.

Are students, parents, educators, school and district leaders, and policymakers ready for this brave new education world? Each stakeholder in the transformation process has an important new role to play. Let's meet the players.

CHAPTER 3

Student Perspective

Students are at the heart of competency-based education and everything we do as educators. They are the reason we give 200 percent of our time and energy. Teachers, administrators, board members, and community members all have common goals to help their students. How this looks can be quite different depending on the stakeholder. Often, they want to help but are not sure how to begin or how to make change in positive ways without compromising what they know works. This chapter is a glimpse into what education might look like from a student's point of view. In our experience, we have seen that students are excited to learn when they see the power of their passions coming alive. In this chapter, we show what a day might look like in the life of a student, both at the primary and secondary levels.

For the youngest students, learning is exciting, and they long to share with others what they have learned. As they grow older, this passion and excitement dwindles. In traditional systems, students are expected to wait for others to understand the lessons and even to refrain from asking too many questions when things don't make sense. Being accepted by others becomes more important than learning what the teacher wants them to learn. Regardless of the type of system they're in, when teachers are able to help students feel safe and accepted, learning takes place for a majority of the students. But even in the best of classrooms in a traditional system, not every student's needs are met, because the system was never intended to do so. Traditional education is to educate a mass of students who meet minimum requirements for passing. Since the conception of education in the United States, adaptations have been made for students with special needs and gifted students, but the same time-bound system is still in place (Center on Education Policy, 2020). In the CBE system, students become part of the system, helping them understand why they are learning the lessons they're learning as well as where they are going with the learning and how it helps them progress toward goals they believe in. When students believe they can make a difference for themselves and others, and that their opinion matters, they begin to participate. Students in the CBE system are excited to learn when they see the power of their passions coming alive. All students' needs are able to be met. It is critical for teachers and leaders to understand the student perspective of CBE for them to best meet these needs.

The essential questions that this chapter covers include the following.

- What are important factors for students in a CBE system?
- For students, how does the CBE system compare to traditional systems?
- What do primary and secondary student perspectives look like in CBE?
- What are the takeaways from this chapter?

What Are Important Factors for Students in a CBE System?

For students to excel in any learning environment, they *need to understand how to navigate the system*. This includes understanding all the critical attributes of a competency-based system. Students need to know that they are safe in the design of the learning environment and are supported when they make mistakes. Students should be able to articulate the vision they have for their learning and how they are supported by their teachers and peers. They should be able to see how to progress as leaders once they are ready and desire to help others. CBE systems measure progress for students in four stages: (1) culture, (2) goals, (3) feedback, and (4) digital platform—see figure 3.1. These components are vital for student success.

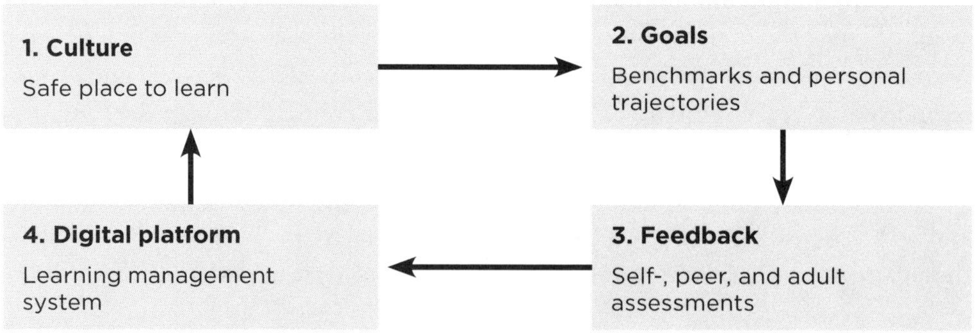

Figure 3.1: CBE student progression stages.

Stage 1: Culture

Students need to feel safe within the culture of their classroom and school. Failure must seem to students like a pathway to success rather than something to fear or a reason for others to make fun of them. Helping every student be secure in their own skin requires intentional lessons on social-emotional learning and well-being. Places to start include Angela Maiers's (TEDx Talks, 2011) work on mattering, Carol S. Dweck's (2016) work on the growth mindset, and the book *The School Wellness Wheel: A Framework Addressing Trauma, Culture, and Mastery to Raise Student Achievement* by Mike Ruyle, Libby Child, and Nancy Dome (2021). Today's students suffer collective trauma and negative impacts on their mental health more than any other generation (Laderer, 2023). As educators, we need to recognize the importance of addressing these emotional and physical needs before we can begin teaching rigor in content areas.

CBE systems begin with a process of creating a culture of collaboration in every classroom, school, and district that is respectful of everyone's needs and makes it possible, once established, for students to have voice and choice on what and how they learn. We call these codes of collaboration (see the Classroom Tools section, page 57). This allows students to feel empowered to take on more responsibility for their own learning.

Here and in the following sections, we include some examples of what you might hear learners think, say, and act like in a CBE system. In other words, we put ourselves, as readers, into the footsteps of learners. Let's wave a magic wand and pretend we are transported into a CBE system of learning. What do you see as a student? What types of activities will you be doing as a student in a CBE system? How is your day different from traditional classroom experiences? You will notice that these statements describe the elements we feel are essential: a code of collaboration for a safe learning environment, voice and choice, pacing that works for individual students' needs, and excitement for learning because of transparency about why it is important and how these learners can progress toward their goals. The students we have worked with and who have seen success with CBE represent a wide variety of racial, cultural, and economic backgrounds. The following student statement is not a direct quote but rather an amalgamation of perspectives gathered from our countless conversations with students in CBE systems:

> *We have individual, group, and whole-class instruction, depending on what my needs are or the unit I am working on. As I gain confidence in my ability and independent learning, I have more choices in what I learn and how I learn it. I have tools and processes to assist me in accomplishing my learning targets. We have standard operating procedures in our classroom to help us be timely, efficient, and productive.*

This statement shows how students are encouraged not only to succeed for themselves but also as a collective:

> *I have responsibility for not only my success, but also my classmates' successes. We monitor all the things that are important to us and try to improve the outcomes when there are delays.*

Stage 2: Goals

Benchmarks and personal trajectories help students build the plan for moving forward at their own pace. The pace should be unique for each student, within reason, and attainable so they can reach their goals. Their pace should not allow them to get frustrated waiting for the whole class to move together or anxious because they feel everyone is waiting for them. In the traditional system, students are broken up by age, and the classroom moves together, some a little faster and some taking more time, but at the end of the unit (three to six weeks or semester-long), students are evaluated based on that time for learning. In a CBE system, students can move at their own pace, and technology helps students and teachers monitor progress, checking and adjusting as needed. The tools and process for establishing this component will take effort and time to put into place, but the rewards are astounding.

Students like to see where they are currently and where they need to go. In working with the students one on one, we have always been amazed at how unrealistic their vision was in believing they could master such a vast amount of work in a short time. The tool in figure 3.2 is an example of a gap analysis spreadsheet, a way to use data to plan each student's trajectory toward high school graduation. This tool allows them to set specific targets and goals that are reasonable and have a say in how they plan to move forward. Thanks to technology, the school's LMS can help students and their teachers manage this more efficiently than individual spreadsheets.

We put this gap analysis process into place at one school for all students who were planning on graduating within two to three years. The tool showed where students currently were in each content area and where they needed to be for graduation. In a student-led meeting, the teacher, the student, a parent or family member, and an advisor would review each of the content areas and the expectations for level completion, then discuss how they could each support the plan. The gap analysis was reviewed regularly—no less than every six weeks—with the students, the teachers, and, if necessary, the parents. A more formal review would be scheduled if students were not on track for graduating according to the plan they developed at the beginning of the year. Because of an online platform that could be viewed by students, families, teachers, advisors, and administration, it was easy to keep track of progress or lack of progress.

This type of data-driven decision making helps students feel more in control of their pace, their projects, and their choice of what to focus on next. Their work centers on

Student Name: Jaye | Advisor: Ms. M

Light gray = done medium gray = on track dark gray = alert | Started in seventh grade

Note: Click on content area to go to remaining standards

Careers		Writing		Mathematics		Personal Social Service		Reading		Science		Social Environments		Technology		total left
Level 3	18	Level 4	38	Level 3	70	Level 5	15	Level 4	23	Level 5	8	Level 5	20	Level 4	11	203

Total Standards Completed	
2006–2007	220
2007–2008	124
2008–2009	119
2009–2010	107

Note: We revised the standards in 2007 from a total of 1,500 to 832.

Pacing for one year = 143 standards
Given rate for graduation = 1.4 years

Note: Color coding is arbitrary and reflects dark gray if not on track for graduation or if there is no progress made over a specific period of time. The period of time may be anywhere from one week to one month, depending on the individual plan.

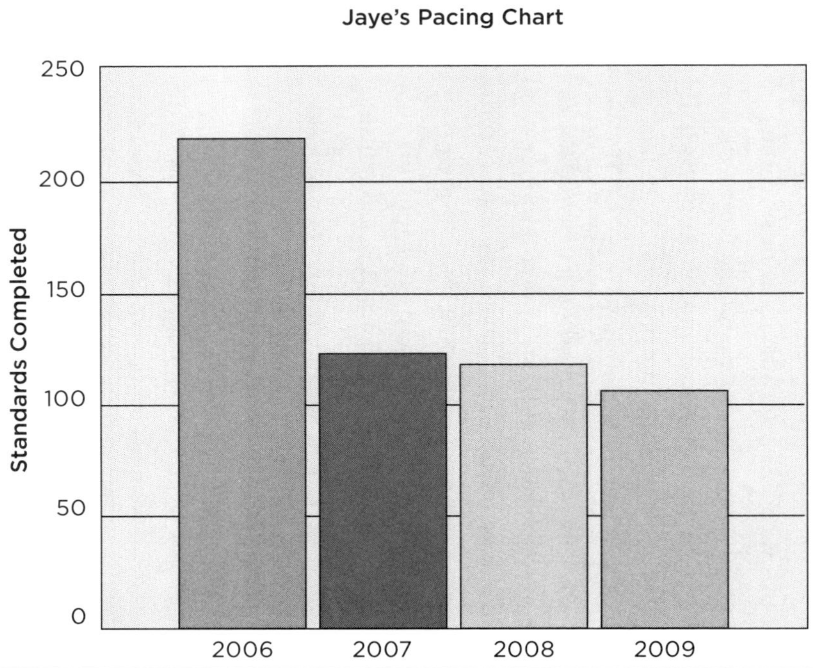

Source: Mourant, 2011.

Figure 3.2: Gap analysis snapshot.

their needs, and they can choose to create a project plan (we called these individual learning plans, or ILPs) to come up with something that they consider cool to learn about that also meets the criteria for the targets they need to master. At first, students need a lot of help creating and implementing their ILPs, but after successfully completing a few, they welcome the opportunity to have more say in what they are learning and choose how they can show mastery. The first steps begin with teacher-led instruction. Units are introduced for a whole class, and students are grouped by like interests or target levels. ILPs are at first for groups and later for individuals, and students can choose them from a playlist the teacher provides with options for variation. Students are also welcome to come up with their own personal ILPs, but at first, the teacher does most of the directing until students are ready to implement their own ILPs with success. Some examples of ILPs are available later in the chapter.

The following student statement boils down perspectives we've heard about working through personal trajectories:

> *When I come into the classroom, I know exactly where I'm at in my learning and if I am on target to reach my goals. My teacher and other adults have included me in the shared vision process so my voice has meaning for what I should be able to know and do. When I begin my lessons, it is at the level that I know I need—a bit challenging, but also attainable—and I have resources to help me along the way. In addition to my teacher, I have my peers, online resources, community members, and of course my family. For example, when I get stuck in math, I often go to Khan Academy online and find relevant videos to explain a concept I am struggling with. For language arts, my teacher allows me to work on a project that uses the writing skills I have been practicing to be proficient in a science fair project. I keep checking my work, looking at the self-assessment tools provided as well as the descriptions of the rubrics online that help me see what a finished product could look like. This type of learning has really helped me see the importance of what I am learning and not get bored like I used to be when I sat in classes waiting for other students to catch up to what we were learning.*

This statement helps show another way that a student might put personal experience to bear in the classroom while achieving benchmarks:

> *I like that I don't always have to sit and wait for the teacher to tell me what to do; but there are different ways for me to work ahead when I already know something or get extra help when I need more practice or clarification. For example, in algebra, we were working with rate conversions in units, but I had just returned from Mexico, where we did everything in metrics, so I showed what I knew, and was able to skip ahead. Our online reporting system lets me see*

what is next and where to go to find the resources to help me be successful, including direct instruction from my teacher.

Stage 3: Feedback

Giving students specific feedback helps encourage them to see the value of effort, rather than just feeling "smart" or "dumb." Using Dweck's (2016) growth mindset can be a powerful tool in helping students understand the power of *yet* and know that they can continue to improve until they are satisfied with the results and are ready for the next step. This notion explains that the difference between a fixed mindset and a growth mindset can make a huge difference in learning. The *growth mindset* is believing that learning is a result of effort rather than inborn ability (Dweck, 2016).

CBE systems include a toolbox of strategies that are customized for each situation. The best strategies will depend on students' needs and what they relate to. For example, Roxanne worked with a robotics team whose members always had some great ideas on how to improve their performance and worked together well to communicate what should be done. For assessments, Roxanne managed to get the team to display their projects each year during the National Engineers Week Anchorage and Alaska Engineer of Year Award conference. In a side room or hallway, engineers would stop in briefly to check out the cool "toys" and ask the students specific questions about how they adapted particular parts. The students knew their information forward and backward since they created it all. They loved the attention and especially loved hearing suggestions for what they might not have thought of. The team helped develop a feedback tool that visiting guests could quickly fill out to contribute to our team reflection later. Since the students helped come up with the tool and the process, they had ownership of how we used it, and they paid attention to the information provided.

Another example is when Roxanne asked her colleagues to do classroom observations. She explained to her students why the guest was in the room and the purpose of their visit. This modeling showed that she, too, was a learner open to constructive feedback in order to improve. Feedback should come in a variety of ways for self-reflection and continuous improvement, whether it's for our learners or for our own classrooms and schools. Teachers model what they expect from students, including professional learning, so every stakeholder (students, families, teachers, noncertified staff, business partners, and decision makers) can practice the processes and gain experience to see when and how to use them in different situations.

This student statement comes from numerous conversations about how students view feedback:

My friends and I don't always get to work together, and I realize that I need to mix it up with independent projects and group work. There are times when others have mastered something and can help me figure out the concept, making me "proficient," and they earn "advanced" standing for teaching someone else. When we check our work, the assessment is always to a very high standard, which makes me feel good about my accomplishments.

Stage 4: Digital Platform

Keeping track of each student's learning within content areas and classrooms can be too much to ask of teachers. It's important to be able to view students' progress from their perspective, from the families' view, from the teacher's view, and from the administrator's view and see how the pacing aligns with personalized goals, strategies, and projects. Each student works on at least five to as many as twenty targets at any given time. Students may be assessed by multiple instructors and have both individual and group projects to show mastery. Having a digital platform is essential in today's complex world of education. There are many examples of schools and districts trying to do this by hand; but for effective interactions for all involved, it requires a complex set of tools that are only possible through a platform that supports a CBE system. There are a variety of learning management systems that assist with this process, but to have the best results, a whole district needs to embrace CBE in order to have a system that will be sustainable.

Lindsay Unified School District (2017) in California documents its shifts to competency-based learning in the book *Beyond Reform*. The digital platform the district uses is a huge part of this change process. The video "A Day in the Life of an Empowered Lindsay Learner" (www.youtube.com/watch?v=QRKnTbkouXA) provides a snapshot of how the digital platform pulls together all aspects of students' academic lives.

For Students, How Does the CBE System Compare to Traditional Systems?

In traditional systems, students wait to be told what to do and guess at the expectations of each teacher. They are masters at playing the game to see what is expected of them to get an A. School can sometimes be fun and engaging, but unfortunately, it's the exception rather than the rule. Even the best traditional systems do not adequately prepare students for success in the real world (XQ Institute, n.d.). Many students find themselves unable to navigate the system of finding meaningful employment or even completing applications for college (Wilbur & Roscigno, 2016). Students who do succeed most often have a parent or advocate who can help them navigate what to expect and how to advance (Wilbur & Roscigno, 2016). School systems today are not set up for every student to succeed. There is little to no consistency among classrooms, districts, or states.

As educators, we are also lifelong learners, and part of our job and obligation is to continually improve to find ways to be more effective. In a traditional system, there is only so far we can go. With CBE, students are advocates for their own learning, giving them opportunities to find their passions and eagerly learn new things. Instead of waiting for teachers to tell them what to do as in a traditional system, students have a clear road map of what they need to know and be able to do. They are able to understand what they're learning and why.

Transitioning from a traditional to a competency-based system takes time and intentional steps. In our decades of experience, we have seen many failures and some success. We have identified key components that successful schools follow to track their progress in implementing CBE. These components make up comprehensive road maps for teachers, schools, and districts, which we unpack in further detail in chapters 4 (page 73), 5 (page 113), and 6 (page 139). Figure 3.3 is a student road map showing how implementation of CBE would look from a student's perspective. This shows what it might sound like for a student if CBE were implemented in four quarters (not necessarily a yearlong timeline but in phases).

The student road map is different from the other stakeholders' road maps because the students don't get the choice of implementing it, although courageous leaders

	School Culture	Benchmarks	Personal Trajectories	Feedback	Digital Platform
First Quarter—Traditional Learning	Students are directed by the teacher in the educational process.	Students do not know how to set goals.	Students do not plan their learning.	Students do not leave feedback.	Not applicable
	Students have no or limited experience with group work.	Extrinsic motivation prevails.		Students may sporadically receive feedback from teacher and classmates.	
	Students lack habits of productive reflection.			Students engage in learning for grades.	
Second Quarter—Start of CBE System	Students periodically demonstrate conscious independence in the classroom.	Students engage in collective goal setting of nonacademic goals.	Students can occasionally work at their own pace in some lessons.	Students leave feedback on teacher's initiative.	Students know basic functionality of the platform.
	Students periodically work in groups.	Achieving collective goals maintains motivation. The role of marks in general remains.	Collective planning of module, with individual choice of tasks, is possible at level 2.0.	Students receive detailed feedback from the teacher.	Students use platform in some lessons.
	Students sporadically engage in productive reflection.				

Figure 3.3: Student road map—Primary and secondary

continued →

<table>
<tr><th></th><th>School Culture</th><th>Benchmarks</th><th>Personal Trajectories</th><th>Feedback</th><th>Digital Platform</th></tr>
<tr><td rowspan="3">Third Quarter—Routine CBE</td><td>Students systematically and proactively demonstrate their autonomy within the framework established by jointly created documents.</td><td>Students set academic goals (with teacher's help).</td><td>Students work at their own pace in lessons.</td><td>Students leave occasional feedback to the teacher on their own initiative.</td><td>Students use the LMS platform to work at their own pace.</td></tr>
<tr><td>Independently or with the help of a teacher, students choose the necessary form of work.</td><td rowspan="2">Students initiate setting personal or nonacademic collective goals.</td><td>Students occasionally create their own trajectory in module.</td><td rowspan="2">Students provide feedback to their classmates (for example, through peer review).</td><td>Students occasionally create their own trajectory.</td></tr>
<tr><td>Reflection leads to setting personal or academic goals (with teacher's help).</td><td>If desired, they can begin with testing tasks at higher levels to see if mastery is already achieved.</td><td>Students use platform every day.</td></tr>
<tr><td rowspan="3">Fourth Quarter—CBE Refinement</td><td>Students are responsible for their learning. They initiate, if necessary, review of jointly created documents.</td><td rowspan="3">Students set personal goals by themselves. They initiate and participate in collective goal setting with the class.</td><td>Students work at their own pace during whole module.</td><td>Students leave feedback for teacher on their own initiative.</td><td>Students freely use the platform in their learning.</td></tr>
<tr><td>Students choose the necessary form of work to achieve their goals.
Students self-assess who they are and how they relate to others.</td><td>Students create their own trajectory in module.</td><td>Students freely and responsibly use peer review.</td><td rowspan="2">Students regularly create their own trajectory.</td></tr>
<tr><td>Students initiate reflection, which leads to setting personal or academic goals.</td><td>Students use freed-up time as they desire.</td><td>Students can objectively assess themselves.</td></tr>
</table>

would include students in the awareness and readiness stages so they have a voice and choice about the change and choosing to support it. The CBE system or traditional system will be what they are in, not what they choose to be in. While students may not have a choice of which system their school uses, CBE implementation means that students can then have a voice in many other areas when they are ready as leaders. The more involved they are, the higher their ownership of the system.

Learning is more than just the basic academic competencies of reading, writing, and arithmetic; it should now include a variety of content areas for the whole child, including social-emotional and personal skills.

Some teachers are able to *flip* their classrooms, a movement started by Jon Bergmann (2022). Flipped classrooms allow for the information students need to learn to be presented through video or other technologies from their teacher where they access them away from the classroom. The time in class is spent with more hands-on experiences with the teacher facilitating the room, rather than standing and delivering information. A flipped classroom is still based in the traditional time-bound system, but it moves toward more hands-on learning with student engagement.

This section charts the progression of CBE implementation in the areas of curriculum, instruction, assessment, reporting, and roles and responsibilities. The charts are simplified from our normal six-stage CBE implementation process to just two (starting and refining) to give a better perspective of where the flipped classroom fits into these ideas. Sometimes, as teachers, we cannot control the whole system, but we can control what happens in our own classroom. This shows what the experience of each of these areas looks and feels like from a student's point of view, from a traditional system (on the left) to making changes to each classroom as they are ready (flipped classroom) to CBE implementation for schools and districts ready to make that change systemwide. More details on these six stages of the CBE road map for classrooms are available in chapter 4 on teacher perspective (page 73).

Figure 3.4 shows how the curriculum would look from a student's view starting with the traditional system (time bound, age-grouped). The traditional view for students is what most classrooms use today, mainly because it's what we know and

Traditional	Flipped Class	CBE Start	CBE Refined
I wait for the teacher to tell me what to do. I'm not sure what we are doing in class. There are some activities that the teacher has us do, but I'm not sure why.	Teacher gives us clear directions about what we will be learning and why. Teacher has choices of resources and projects. Much of the class time is used for hands-on practice of what we are learning.	There's a clear road map on what I need to know and be able to do. I have voice and choice on what my projects are.	I have more choice in directing my learning on things that are important to me. I have opportunities to be part of the student leadership that helps drive curriculum for our district.
Curriculum			

Figure 3.4: CBE progression on curriculum—Student view.

are able to do. Some teachers are masters at engaging students, but the system itself does not meet the needs of all students because it is not set up to do that. If you were to visit a classroom and ask the students what they were learning about the curriculum, the chart shows what you might expect to hear them say. In the flipped classroom, students are much more engaged with hands-on learning, since the teacher delivers direct instruction through video that students access before they come into the classroom. They already have the background information and now are ready to understand at a deeper level through testing the theories themselves. At the CBE start, the classroom has moved beyond flipping to a system that is no longer time bound. The learning is constant, and time is the variable. What students learn is consistent, but how long it takes may vary. Also, in a CBE system, all learning outcomes and expectations are transparent. There's no guessing about what is going to be learned and why. Students have more choices on how they master the material. At first, teachers provide the choices, but as students are more involved and understand they can provide input, those choices expand, with teacher approval, as students are ready for more responsibility.

When they give instruction in traditional systems, the teachers are expected to know all the answers. They are *sages on the stage* who need to share their knowledge and expertise with their students. Having highly qualified teachers is a concept that goes hand in hand with being a professional. No matter what system you teach in, you should know your content. However, as we progress to the right on the chart in figure 3.5, you'll see a shift from the teacher being the center of all information to students now discovering the answers through their hands-on experiences. Teachers are still very knowledgeable, but they act more as facilitators, helping guide the discussion and learning toward the end goals.

Assessments are wonderful tools when used for learning. In traditional systems (see figure 3.6), most assessments are at specific points of the calendar or at the end

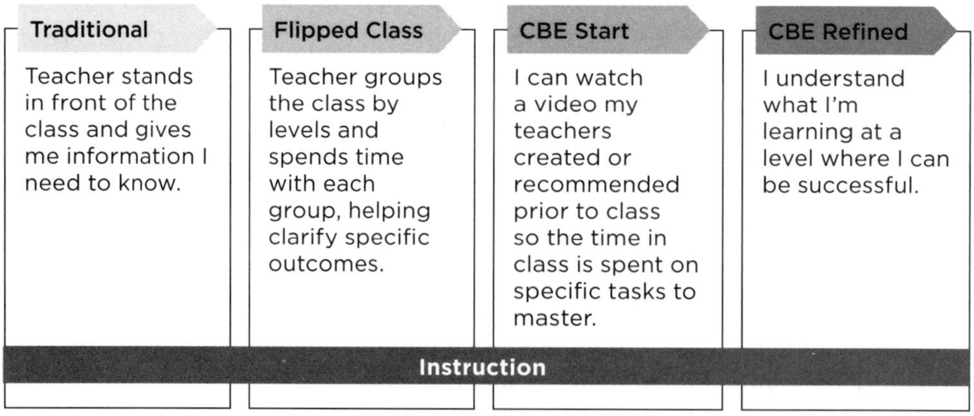

Figure 3.5: CBE progression on instruction—Student view.

Traditional	Flipped Class	CBE Start	CBE Refined
I wait for the teacher to give me a test based on what we just learned.	I have multiple ways to assess myself in preparation for the teacher's test based on what we just learned.	I know where to find assessments to show mastery for each standard I must master.	With voice and choice, I can demonstrate proficiency in a variety of ways.
Assessment			

Figure 3.6: CBE progression on assessment—Student view.

of a unit to prove how much or little the student has retained. As we move toward the right side, you'll see a variety of assessments that are used to measure how each target is mastered and what gaps students still need to work on. Teachers administer assessments as the students are ready.

Once again, the chart in figure 3.7 shows the flow from time bound (traditional) to reporting as progress is made. In CBE systems, there is an LMS that helps track progress and trajectories. Reporting becomes transparent for all stakeholders. Students can see anytime what they need to work on and celebrate what they have mastered. Parents or caregivers can verify and encourage their children. Teachers and administrators can personalize the instruction needed and see trend data to help make better decisions for individual students, classrooms, and whole buildings.

In traditional education, teachers are the main rule givers (see figure 3.8, page 54). In elementary classrooms, students often compete for the honor of having an additional responsibility that the teacher allows. As we grow older, students give up the extra responsibilities to focus more on social standing. In a CBE system, students are part of the process and provide a huge impact on how the system can improve to

Traditional	Flipped Class	CBE Start	CBE Refined
I receive a report card four times a year. I get a progress report every few weeks.	I lead my parents through student-led conferences to show my learning progress each quarter.	I am able to explain what I have learned each week based on evidence.	I have a real-time, digital profile that tracks my progress on my learning.
Reporting			

Figure 3.7: CBE progression on reporting—Student view.

Traditional	Flipped Class	CBE Start	CBE Refined
Sometimes I follow the rules given to me by my teacher. I keep my hands to myself sometimes and try to listen to my teacher.	I get the rules from my teacher, and I monitor my progress.	I set goals and make changes, if needed, for my behavior. I have a voice in the vision of our class and how we are going to work with each other. We monitor our goals.	I am responsible for my behavior and help support others on their journey. I meet my goals and deadlines and have sped up my learning. We continually make adjustments to monitor our behavior in the classroom.
Roles and Responsibilities			

Figure 3.8: CBE progression on roles and responsibilities—Student view.

better meet the needs of all students. Their perspective is valued in processes that not only allow for their participation but require it for quality input.

What Do Primary and Secondary Student Perspectives Look Like in CBE?

In a CBE system, students don't have to wait to be told what to do. They can learn through various experiences, tools, and processes that the teachers have made available to them. As students become more self-directed, they are able to help with finding meaningful projects and community partners who help them engage in real change and not just classroom simulations. Following are some examples of what a day in the life might look like in a CBE system for both primary and secondary students. Both examples are real students, but some of the story has been modified to include components of a CBE system that include multiple students' experiences. These stories help shed light on what a day might look like from a student's viewpoint, both elementary and secondary. We begin with Roven, who, at nine years old, would be in fourth grade in a traditional system:

> *Roven started this year in a CBE classroom that is much different from last year's traditional classroom. He was excited to see his goals and learning plan for the week after working so hard last week on his project about the planets. His group struggled at first*

to understand what each person was responsible for. However, using the process they had reviewed with their teacher, they were able to get through the hard part and really have fun putting together a 3-D model of our solar system that lit up and was pretty impressive. It wasn't their first attempt, either. Roven was surprised at the feedback their team got from the other teams when they first presented their ideas. The other students suggested specific changes that made a huge difference in their final product. Last year, Roven dreaded going to school because he felt so awkward and wondered what to do and say when he arrived before the teacher had taken roll call and started the daily routine.

Today, as he entered the classroom, Roven checked the wall chart for what he needed to have ready when class started. Once he had gathered his supplies and put them on top of the table where he and three other students worked together, he saw that his favorite morning activity, the 3-D puzzles, was already taken. As much as he liked to solve the puzzles, he also enjoyed the other two choices, so he started in the reading corner with the book he selected that was challenging to read. His teacher had shown him how to use sentences around the tough words to understand the meaning, so he didn't mind that it was a bit harder than he was used to. He remembered last year, when he had tough books, how frustrated he would get, even to the point of throwing his book down hard and getting in trouble. It was great to learn strategies for reading but also how to recognize his emotions and what to do when he felt like giving up. His mind raced to the phrase, "I don't have it . . . yet." He giggled as he visualized the flying hero who never let his self-talk be negative, using the strategy he learned for self-correcting.

This year felt so much different. He was more mature, yes, but the classroom was a place he felt safe. He could try things and not feel like an idiot in front of the other students. Last year he acted out a lot, but thankfully most of his bad scores in conduct only showed up at the end of the quarter. It was easier to not deal with it. This year, his teacher recognized some of the signs right away and helped him work through how to be more confident in a nice way. He liked this teacher. He would try even harder now on the next project.

Jade's story, which follows, is an example of a CBE system in remote Alaska, where many students learn in blended environments. Their schools are small, with just five to fifteen high school students in some villages, so they collaborate online with other communities to share teachers, resources, and projects. Jade would traditionally be a junior in high school, but he is actually at different levels for different content areas because of his ILP. Jade is Roxanne's nephew; his story is embellished with some experiences from some of her other students to give examples of what a day might look like for a high school student.

> *Jade brushed off the snow and hung things to dry when his curiosity got the best of him: How does the ice flow impact the migration of seals? Now that he had shot his first seal and given it to his umma, he realized how little he really knew about his surroundings, even though he had grown up on the tiny island of Diomede, Alaska. As he settled into his room that he shared with his two brothers and occasionally with his little sister, who was starting to wander everywhere, Jade opened Google on his laptop to search for more information on seals. His curiosity drove his passion to learn. The hours flew by as he learned about why the seals migrated, why they had become endangered, and what laws had changed to protect them so that he could once again hunt them now as his ancestors had for centuries. He was glad his teacher had a flipped classroom that allowed a lot of individual work to be done in his home where he was relaxed and could spend time diving into things he was interested in, then do activities around the learning targets in class with his peers. It made school much more hands-on for him.*
>
> *It was getting late, but he realized he should get credit for this learning. He logged onto the learning management system and checked out the required classes he still needed to finish for high school graduation. The color dashboard he had customized with his avatar brought up quickly the numerous classes he had mastered, and showed him five more that he still had to address. Under each was a link to numerous choices of which way he wanted to do this—several courses to choose from for each of the multiple intelligences categories. Some were web-based, some were face-to-face with the new teacher who had arrived at Diomede this fall, and some were a combination of web-video and contact with the instructor throughout the five-week course.*
>
> *He located the advanced biology class that he could begin working on through the research he was interested in around the study of seals. Jade noticed lots of links to experts in the field, scientists who had published journals and articles around the topic and who were available via instant message to answer questions online. He also saw examples of other students' projects to give him ideas of how he might eventually design a project to show mastery to the instructor online. Jade decided to start by emailing the instructor in Nome, the next village over with the science teacher, to be sure he understood what the course involved and to know if he could do it without a highly qualified teacher on-site, but a mathematics*

teacher who could oversee his work there. His mathematics teacher was from Wales (the nearby village), and he knew him well; this teacher would be really excited to work with him—he was sure.

We believe the journey for students should begin with establishing a safe environment for learning. This means they have a voice and choice on what is happening in the classroom and they can use tools to show mastery without waiting for the teacher to instruct them on each point. Administrators must support their teachers by ensuring they are proficient at setting up a safe classroom environment and all expectations are consistent throughout their buildings, whether it's face-to-face or virtual. Students need to feel valued. Incorporating social-emotional strategies into daily routines eliminates most of the discipline challenges and gives students a sense of pride in their work and who they are. Here we discuss some classroom tool examples, critical pieces of the CBE student experience that are non-negotiable, and lessons learned.

Classroom Tools

Students who are engaged understand why they are learning the day's lessons. They can connect learning to specific outcomes in their reporting tools and explain it to their peers and families. Students must feel safe, and addressing social-emotional wellness is critical to begin to establish a relationship where students feel they can take risks for learning challenging lessons and not fear ridicule. That's why we recommend starting with classroom culture.

This section contains examples of tools that can be used in a CBE classroom. These tools reflect the elements of CBE. For example, levels of performance are inherent in them—*I need help*, *I can almost do it*, and *I can do it* for elementary students and *Emerging*, *Developing*, *Proficient*, and *Advanced* for secondary students. They start with culture, norms, and behavior and progress to academic outcomes.

Teachers will gain students' trust when they give students a voice and a choice on what they want their environment to look like, feel like, sound like, and act like. By setting them up for success, you will engage the whole class in dialogue, ensuring all voices are heard and honored. Walking through a process, students will create what they feel the four to five rules of class (we call it a code of collaboration) should be (Marzano, Norford, Finn, & Finn, 2017). Then, each day (or as often as needed), the students will help facilitate assessing the class on how well they are doing and which rule needs to be improved.

It's important to be clear about what a code of collaboration is and what it is not. The code of collaboration identifies and lists appropriate behaviors and traits, but it is *not* a dictated set of rules. To achieve this, teachers should collect input from students. For example, to connect with class vision, the teacher might ask students the following questions.

- "What qualities does a successful learner have?"
- "What does good learning look, sound, and feel like?"
- "How do team players act, think, and feel?"

The teacher leads the whole class through an activity of what they want their class to look like, feel like, and act like. The following process is useful.

- Break into small groups (five to seven people).
- Brainstorm what you want your group to look like, feel like, and sound like.
    - List *all* ideas (no comments when taking them; one idea spurs another).
    - Make sure you've gone around the group until there's no more ideas out there.
    - Group like ideas.
    - If needed, power vote on the top three to five items.
    - Agree, as a group, that all will support the final outcome, and refer to it often. (It's OK to disagree, but once a decision is made, everyone sticks to it.)
- Narrow down list to five to fifteen items.

The final product, after grouping and ensuring all voices are heard, is to put up a poster that the class can use for a reminder and daily self-assessment. See figure 3.9 for an example of a code of collaboration in a secondary class with a glimpse at the process of creating it. Figures 3.10 (page 61) and 3.11 (page 61) show two examples of simple finished codes of collaboration you might see in a typical classroom.

With each of these tools, the objective is to have the whole group feel an ownership over the environment where they have a say in how it looks like, feels like, and acts like. Practicing these processes and tools gives experience for situations to recognize what tool might aid the efficiency of the task to be completed in a fair and successful manner.

Sliding Scale				Code of Collaboration				Retreat 2009
¡QUE BIEN! = Tu	¡EXCELENTE! = W	¡BRAVO! = Th	¡BUEN TRABAJO! = F	* A *	+ P +	√ D √	- E -	* **Advanced** • Expertise • Teach others • Present
1. Mutual respect					¡QUE BIEN!			
2. Constructive criticism					¡QUE BIEN!			
3. Specific takeaways (ideas, advice, tools, examples				¡QUE BIEN!				+ **Proficient** • Mastery • Applying
4. "Own" our decisions						¡QUE BIEN!		
5. Voice uncertainties and disagreements					¡QUE BIEN!			

Figure 3.9: Code of collaboration example—Secondary.

continued →

6. Honor all viewpoints					√ **Developing** • Room for improvement • Practicing
7. Honor the tools and processes					
8. Active listening					
9. Practice kindness					- **Emerging** • Not quite there • Still trying • Getting started
10. Appropriate humor and fun					
11. Positive attitude					
12. Creative energy					

Code of Collaboration

- We will . . .
  - Be respectful to ourselves and others
  - Pause before speaking to answer: it is helpful
  - Turn in our homework when we walk in
  - Put away our chairs and pick up papers before leaving
  - Notice someone doing something good and compliment them

Figure 3.10: Code of collaboration example—Secondary.

Source: Jessica Enderson and Madeline Enderson. Used with permission.

Figure 3.11: Code of collaboration example—Primary.

In figure 3.12 (page 62), elementary students are able to engage immediately to see what they could be doing. For younger students who aren't ready to read yet, this chart just has graphics, but uses the same idea. Often, students don't know what they should be doing, so they sit and wait for the teacher to instruct them. Primary students are used to being told what to do, and secondary students are highly affected by peer pressure and not wanting to stand out, so they wait. This simple tool allows students to be empowered in their environment and make choices that will help them start on a positive note.

Check Yourself!

Morning Jobs

Did you . . .	Yes	No
• Say hello to the teacher?		✓
• Put your stuff into your lockers?	✓	
• Lunch count?	✓	
• Turn in tote and homework?	✓	
• Check your job?		✓
• Check a chair?	✓	
• Sharpen two pencils?		✓
• Go to the bathroom?	✓	
• Fill up your water bottle?	✓	
• Do morning work?	✓	
• Do something nice for someone?	✓	

Figure 3.12: Daily checklist—Primary.

Figure 3.13 is another example of a simple but very effective idea. Having real photos is often a draw for students; they like seeing themselves and their friends up on display. They also act as a rubric to show students still learning to read what teachers expect. Making the expectations crystal clear and transparent is vital for good classroom management.

Figure 3.14 (page 64) is another example of individualizing the lesson. Students love to see when they are making progress and have the attention catching them at good behavior. Instead of written rubrics, younger students may use pictures and have a whole-class discussion at first to talk about what is expected and why. The conversation allows students to see that it's OK when we make mistakes, and we all will be learning together. It helps them to see their own trend data and that others also struggle with being consistent. It normalizes that struggle that we each feel and allows them to start fresh each time, realizing that we will keep practicing.

Walking in a Line		
We need help.	We can almost do it.	We can do it!

How did we do today?		

Figure 3.13: Self-assessment—Primary.

This same type of progress chart can be used for secondary students but with more age-appropriate language and images. Students need clear expectations and affirmation when they are making progress. We are confident that this process is good for all students, not just those with behavior challenges. This process also works well for students who typically excel at school and need to push themselves out of their comfort areas and find ways to grow personally.

Once the culture has been established, educators and students move into other areas beyond the classroom daily habits, and find ways students can be independently checking themselves in writing, reading, mathematics, and so on. Figure 3.15 (page 65) shows another example of self-assessment for writing with student exemplars to show what each level of the rubric looks like. It is a simple rubric but allows students to know, before they start, what is expected. Students will use this to self-assess, sharing what score they expect to receive and why. This opens the conversation with their teacher, who uses the same rubric or scoring guide.

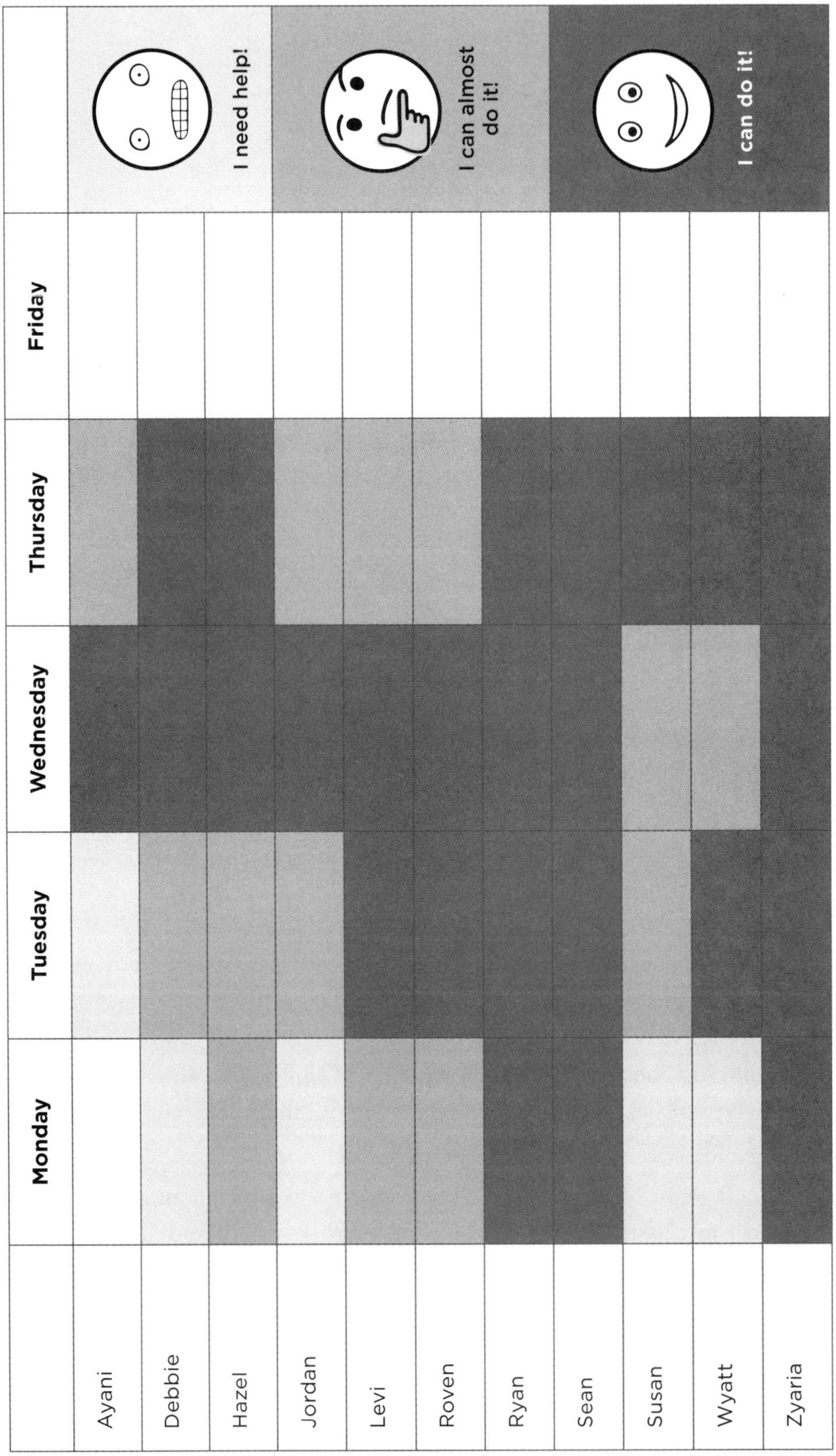

Figure 3.14: Social-emotional learning self-assessment—Primary.

Writing Rubric		

1	**2**	**3**
Date and name Sentence • No pencil • Few words • Missing spaces • Not going left to right Picture • Scribbling (messy) • No details • No colors	Date and Name Sentence • Missing spaces • Picture • Coloring out of the lines • No details	Date and name Sentence • Capitols • Space • Describes Picture • Colored in lines • Details

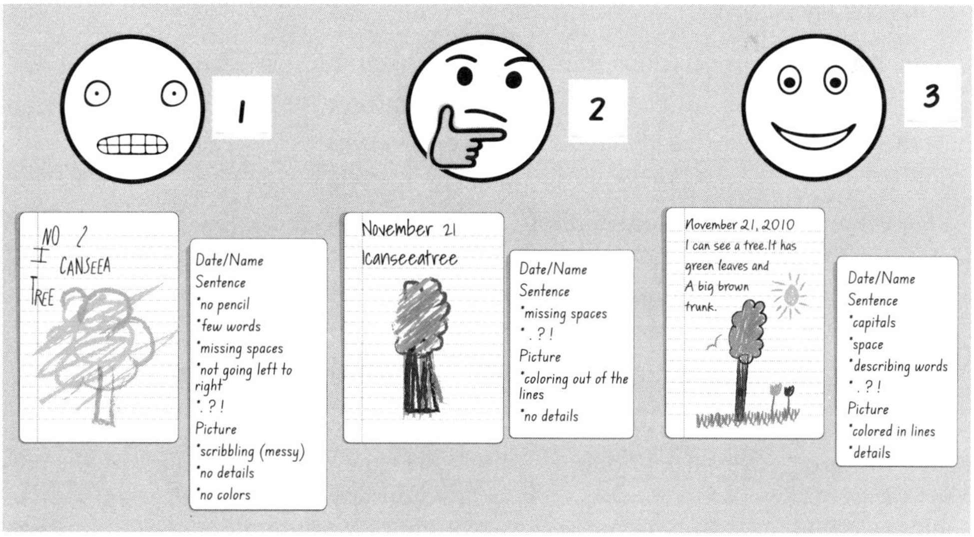

Figure 3.15: Primary self-assessment writing rubric with student exemplars.

All scoring guides should be written in language that anyone can understand, whether it's from a student's perspective, a family member's perspective, a teacher's perspective, and so on. Once students start using the transparent rubrics, it's not the teacher who is scoring the students; students can see for themselves what needs to be done.

Good teaching practices have a balance of different types of instruction as the situation changes. For example, when students are presented with new information, teachers begin with an anticipatory set. This opens their minds for curiosity of what is coming. Once students have the opening activity, they are ready for direct instruction (often used in flipped classrooms as pre-homework). This is the information background needed to move forward with a lesson. Teachers model what they are teaching and practice with the whole group before breaking into smaller groups and then individuals when they are ready.

For example, before taking on a job-shadow project, students would spend several days in class learning what job shadows are and why they are important. Once they have figured out the power and fun of going on field trips to explore different careers, they practice interviewing with each other, taking notes, listening, using body language to communicate appropriate behaviors, and learning about the business before they ever step foot into the location where the job shadow takes place.

Figure 3.16 is an example of what high school students might use when setting up a job shadow for the day or week. It is designed to go alongside the direct instruction of helping students see what they need to do to prepare adequately.

The scale makes expectations transparent—broken into bite-size sections for students to digest—before, during, and after the event. Most students want to jump right into the activity, so having the expectations up front helps set realistic expectations about what they are prepared for (or not) before they experience success or failure. Some of Roxanne's most successful job shadows have been in places where students had decided beforehand that they never wanted to do that particular job. What better way to discover likes and dislikes than before four or more years of college?

Special Education Needs

Students with learning disabilities are usually familiar with the individual learning plan (ILP) process. Similar to their existing individualized education plans, the collaboration of adult experts, teachers, students, and parents covers a variety of content areas and emotional support. In our experience, students in special education fit right into our existing CBE system since educators create individual plans for every student no matter what "label" they may have. The CBE system starts where the learner is currently and builds a personal trajectory based on their passions and lifestyle. Learners have a say in what they are learning and why.

	Advanced	**Proficient**	**Developing**	**Emerging**
Prior to the Experience (Preparation)	☐ Articulately, confidently, and positively states purpose and expectations of the job-shadow experience ☐ Seeks additional information on site by researching and asking in-depth questions prior to experience	☐ Understands purpose and value of job shadow and can convey to others ☐ Prepares three questions ready to ask on site ☐ Has materials and is prompt (pen, paper, questions, and so on). ☐ Obtains all necessary information	☐ Understands at least one purpose of job shadow ☐ Needs assistance from facilitator to think of three questions to ask the job-shadow host ☐ Is on time most of the time and is prepared with most of the necessary materials	☐ Does not listen to introductory information and requirements ☐ Does not prepare questions for site host ☐ Does not have necessary materials and is late
During the Experience	☐ Requests to be more involved (hands-on work) and shows capability to do this ☐ Takes notes that include impressions and facts ☐ Asks all prepared questions articulately and with interest, expanding when appropriate ☐ Displays exemplary pre-employment and interpersonal skills	☐ Introduces self upon meeting host ☐ Asks thoughtful, relevant questions and is actively involved during visit ☐ Dress, manners, and attitude reflect positively on student and program ☐ Records factual notes ☐ Conveys interest in site (eye contact, smile, affirmations, respectful comments)	☐ Is hesitant with introductions—waits until host introduces first ☐ Uses inconsistent eye contact with host or shows lack of interest ☐ Shows willing interest and participates in conversation some of the time ☐ Asks questions that are unclear or have already been answered in conversation	☐ Displays lack of respect for presenter (not paying attention, putting others down, fidgeting, laughing, and so on) or lacks enthusiasm ☐ Does not participate in discussions or ask questions ☐ Gives little or no response to host's questions ☐ Dresses inappropriately
After the Experience (Reflection)	☐ Writes reflection that covers what student learned, relevance to life, possible further exploration, and so on ☐ Writes, checks, revises, and sends grammatically correct and articulate thank-you letter with personal specifics	☐ Completes required reflection in a quality manner ☐ In reflection, conveys to others what student learned ☐ Writes, requests editing, revises, and sends a professional thank-you letter to site host	☐ Attempts to share what student learned, but lacks clarity or a relevant connection to student's own life ☐ Some effort put forth, but does not or cannot write a professional thank-you letter	☐ Refuses to complete reflection or share it with others or does not understand the reflection process ☐ Does not create an effective thank-you letter

Figure 3.16: Job-shadow student self-assessment—Secondary.

Lessons Learned

When making changes in a classroom, a school, or even a whole district, the start of something different may be effective at first simply because there's passion behind teaching in a different way. With CBE, it is tempting to pick and choose what elements to begin with that feel comfortable and you know can be successful. For example, it might be easy to start thematic units if you have not already tried them. It's fun to have a theme that creates excitement and engaging activities, but in their enthusiasm to create amazing projects with students, teachers may overlook some of the other pieces that can make or break the effort.

One example of this from Roxanne's experience is a group trip her students took. One of the school's student groups worked all year to earn money to travel to Washington, DC, and see the monuments in person. After months of events, activities, and fundraising, they finally earned enough to make it possible. It should have been the trip of a lifetime; many of the students had never left their community before. It turned out to be a huge disappointment to many because of the bickering and poor social skills the students exhibited while traveling together. Roxanne quickly realized her mistake of not engaging students to form a group of decision makers who valued each other and of not helping them collaborate to put processes in place to solve conflict before things turned ugly.

You probably have had similar experiences with some teaching units or events that you thought would be amazing but turned sour in the end. The same goes for implementing a complex CBE system. Student engagement and collaboration are pieces that are critical if you want to ensure success. That's why we emphasize a road map that takes into consideration your own individual needs and community before moving forward. We insist on just that for students before they begin a new project—to start with what they already know and what they need to move forward before creating an ILP for them. In the CBE road map, there are considerations for each of the stakeholders who can implement it, including the teacher, principal, and superintendent.

From the students' perspective, we focus on the critical pieces of engagement and collaboration. Over the years of doing CBE, we have found that student apathy is a huge barrier, especially for students who have not had success or face barriers in school. If you do nothing except try to increase student engagement and collaboration, this will lead to much better academic results and fewer disciplinary problems. The CBE system is designed to give students more voice and choice. However, it's critical for teachers to understand that this voice and choice is released over time, depending on when students are ready.

Consider how you would like your students to respond as you start to implement your own CBE system. The following chart (figure 3.17) shows some examples of

Area of CBE System	Question	Student Response
Student engagement: Why positive social-emotional learning is transformative in a CBE classroom	What was the highlight?	• There were choices based on my interests. • Expectations were clear in how to demonstrate proficiency. • There were multiple resources available when I got stuck.
	What was a challenge?	• There was not enough time. • I couldn't understand the rubric. • It's not like what I am used to.
	What can we improve?	• Have it ready before I come to school so I know what to expect. • Be part of our digital platform. • Allow me to show I've learned something.
Student collaboration	How can students collaborate?	• Peer feedback is quick and consistent. • Provide specific ideas of what next steps might be. • Practice together.

Figure 3.17: Student feedback examples—Secondary.

typical student responses regarding their engagement and collaboration. This is one of the CBE process tools for voice and choice and refinement.

Doing what you know works well for students is not always popular or easy. Often, we have seen political jealousy, with naysayers not wanting to look bad themselves and willing to sabotage others who are doing the work. CBE strategies, such as creating codes of collaboration, using learning targets and scoring guides to make lessons relevant and transparent, offering a variety of resources and pathways for students to demonstrate mastery and reach their goals, and enacting processes to guide students toward the next step in their learning, can make the classroom a positive and satisfying place for both students and the teacher. That means teachers can focus on what is best for their students and make progress as quickly as they are comfortable. Building trust with students and helping them recognize they have a voice and choice that really matters helps teachers create an environment where students can be successful as they productively struggle to learn together and be encouraged by one another. Discipline issues in this sort of environment dwindle, and excitement builds for learning. Administrators who recognize the positive change will be supportive.

In CBE systems, one of the lessons we've learned is about the power of student leadership. Students are prepared to be leaders as part of the process. As with any other part of the CBE system, student leaders must have clear expectations. Just like teachers do for students in a classroom, they first provide an anticipatory set to get students ready for what is coming (choosing student leaders) and then provide enough instruction that they are ready to start practicing the tools. Each of the variables for student leadership is situational and can change the way leaders make decisions. Teachers can help students understand that being a leader requires observation of the situation. The research from Ken Blanchard on situational leadership can help educators understand what this looks like, divided into four styles (Hersey, Blanchard, & Johnson, 2013).

1. In the **directive style,** followers have high needs and low commitment risk. The directive style works well when the other students are unskilled with no experience. Their commitment risk is low because they want to learn and are willing to take direction from another student. The student leader can then be directive.
2. When needs and commitment risk are both high, the **coaching style** is appropriate. The other students have some skills and some experience but need coaching to be consistent and competent. Their commitment risk is high because they are unmotivated and will need coaching to help them share in the vision of what they can accomplish.
3. The **supporting style** is useful when the other students demonstrate they have the skills and experience to get the task done (low needs) but lack the confidence to ensure success (high commitment risk). Supporting the other students allows the student leader to take advantage of the skills in the group while motivating everyone to work together as a team to succeed together.
4. Lastly, a student leader can use the **delegating style** when the other students are competent, skilled, experienced, and willing to do tasks without being told. Needs and commitment risk are both low. The job of the leader in this situation is to help monitor the group's progress and keep everyone on task for the greater good of the group by delegating tasks.

Student leaders tend to be directive because it's easier to just tell everyone what to do; however, students who can balance all four styles see that in different situations, they may want to allow others to share their leadership and still be highly effective as a leader. The goal is to have groups who can have a delegating leader, but often it takes time to recognize the situation, the team that is present, and how to get them from where they are to where they can be. As students have guided practice, they will gain confidence and trust in the system, knowing that their presence makes a difference.

What Are the Takeaways From This Chapter?

The CBE system approach is characterized by passion about students having the opportunity to learn in meaningful ways and conviction that *all* students deserve this experience. We want to model what we are dishing out: providing support and vision, starting where each student is at, moving forward with intention, celebrating successes, and learning from mistakes.

CBE has several important factors that help ensure a student-centered, personalized experience. The comparison with the traditional education system reveals key differences in everything from curriculum to the roles and responsibilities of teachers and students themselves. Classroom tools such as codes of collaboration, self-assessments, and rubrics with clear expectations provide students with multiple opportunities to engage with and collaborate on content, knowledge, and skills acquisition. Student leadership is an essential facet of the student perspective in the CBE classroom.

CHAPTER 4

Teacher Perspective

Change is never easy, especially in a system that has been in place for over 150 years and that we defend—even when we know it doesn't work—because it is all we know.

Committed teachers are the essential glue that binds all educational goals together. Their impact—either good or bad—will last a lifetime for their students. Good teachers are passionate about making a difference in their students' lives, or they would have chosen a different profession. If you are reading this book, you may be a leader looking for ways to help your teachers improve their skills, their classrooms, and ultimately their students' opportunities. We would like to help teachers be even more effective practitioners in revolutionary ways that are essential to ensure the long-term success of their students. There are many examples of strategies to integrate competency-based learning into the classroom, but we have found few that address a whole-system approach. In addition to teachers' classroom success, we are equally passionate about the success of schools, districts, states, and countries. To approach CBE in a systematic way, evidence is overwhelming that it begins with teachers and their pivotal role in the lives of their students (Khan, Khan, Zia-Ul-Islam, & Han, 2017). In this chapter, we will share some of the best practices and invite you to consider some strategies that help teachers allow for learning to be constant and time to be the variable.

The essential questions that this chapter answers include the following.

- What are the important factors for teachers in a CBE system?
- For teachers, how does the CBE system compare to traditional systems?
- What do primary and secondary teacher perspectives look like in CBE?
- What does the teacher road map to CBE implementation look like?
- What are the takeaways from this chapter?

What Are the Important Factors for Teachers in a CBE System?

As you consider moving from a traditional, time-bound system of education toward a competency-based system, we feel there are factors that teachers must believe if they are to succeed. These factors are based on years of experience watching teachers who are very different either succeed or quit out of frustration and analyzing their experiences. In Alaska, where we started, many of the teachers were open to sharing their experiences, both good and bad, with us to help us form our opinions for success. The three factors we believe are critical for CBE to work well include (1) believing that all students can learn, (2) embracing research-based change with proven strategies, and (3) acting as leaders throughout the process of implementing and maintaining a CBE system.

Factor 1: Believe That All Students Can Learn

Starting with that non-negotiable moral purpose, we can share openly our heartfelt and outcome-driven efforts for the lifelong success of our students to show firmly that we care and are willing to do whatever it takes to see them succeed. Eradicating failure as an educational outcome means changing our system from a traditional, time-based, industrial model to a more collaborative, inquisitive model where we are facilitators guiding our students down paths that will be unique to them and to us.

Here again we invoke the notion of the growth mindset (Dweck, 2016), an essential mindset for teachers to successfully implement CBE. Teachers must believe that their students are all full of potential, like seeds, ready to grow into their own unique selves. The same is true about education staff. It is easy to dismiss ideas because you are not good in an area; however, we want to model for students that we may not be good *yet* but are willing to give it a try. As leaders, you can help your teachers by providing them with specific encouraging instructional strategies that they can use immediately, one step at a time, as they are ready. Classroom observations should be a welcome activity where teachers see the relationship as win-win rather than judging their ability. Another idea for leaders is to set up peer observations so teachers can help each other and learn from each other. This type of collaboration takes a while to build into because it requires a certain level of trust and respect among all staff members. Building the culture of collaboration with adults should model what we expect from the students. Leaders need to intentionally work on recognizing the strengths each team member brings and help them build their confidence as they work on areas that may be more challenging.

In a CBE system, students have a large role in their own learning. Teachers become more like facilitators and coaches, inspiring their learning. Students can help monitor and self-direct. Teachers are more responsible to ensure students learn and guide them along pathways that make that possible. As leaders, your role is parallel to that of teachers as you help monitor and guide them as they are ready for more responsibility and new strategies. Specific steps of how leaders can support teachers, students, and others are found in chapter 5 (page 113).

Factor 2: Embrace Research-Based Change With Proven Strategies

After agreeing on our moral purpose, enacting substantive change is the single biggest challenge we face. Throughout our own experience in thinking outside the box in changing systems, we have learned that no single tweak to the operational platform and dynamics of our current classrooms will be highly successful. Change is an explosive, frightening event to grapple with, and the reluctance to look foolish—or, worse, to compromise or negatively affect our students' future—can be daunting to those who must make hard decisions. At the end of the day, though, you will see student engagement and know that putting the students' needs first will give everyone the courage to change.

We must never embrace change for change's sake but instead use the very best practices that are now proven road maps and embrace what we need to do differently to keep up with the times. A wise teacher routinely seeks feedback and guidance from respected colleagues and peers. Before launching into a CBE classroom, you must ask yourself if you are really ready for fundamental change to your learning environment and what that might look like.

Best practices should also have deep wells of research to support them. Robert J. Marzano is one of the leading educational research experts. He has written about numerous strategies and practices that are research-based and can be trusted to help you succeed. One place to look is the website www.marzanoresources.com, which is full of resources. *Teaching in a Competency-Based Elementary School* (Marzano & Abbott, 2022) and *Teaching in a Competency-Based Secondary School* (Marzano, Aschoff, & Avila, 2022) are a good place to start. As teachers, we are all required to keep our certificates current. Participating in collaborative teams that focus on reading and discussing the latest research not only meets requirements for recertification; it is also an opportunity to keep abreast with new strategies and trends.

Factor 3: Act as Leaders While Implementing and Maintaining a CBE System

Successful teachers in a CBE system tend to share a number of traits. These are qualities that teachers can develop. Figure 4.1 (page 76) summarizes these characteristics.

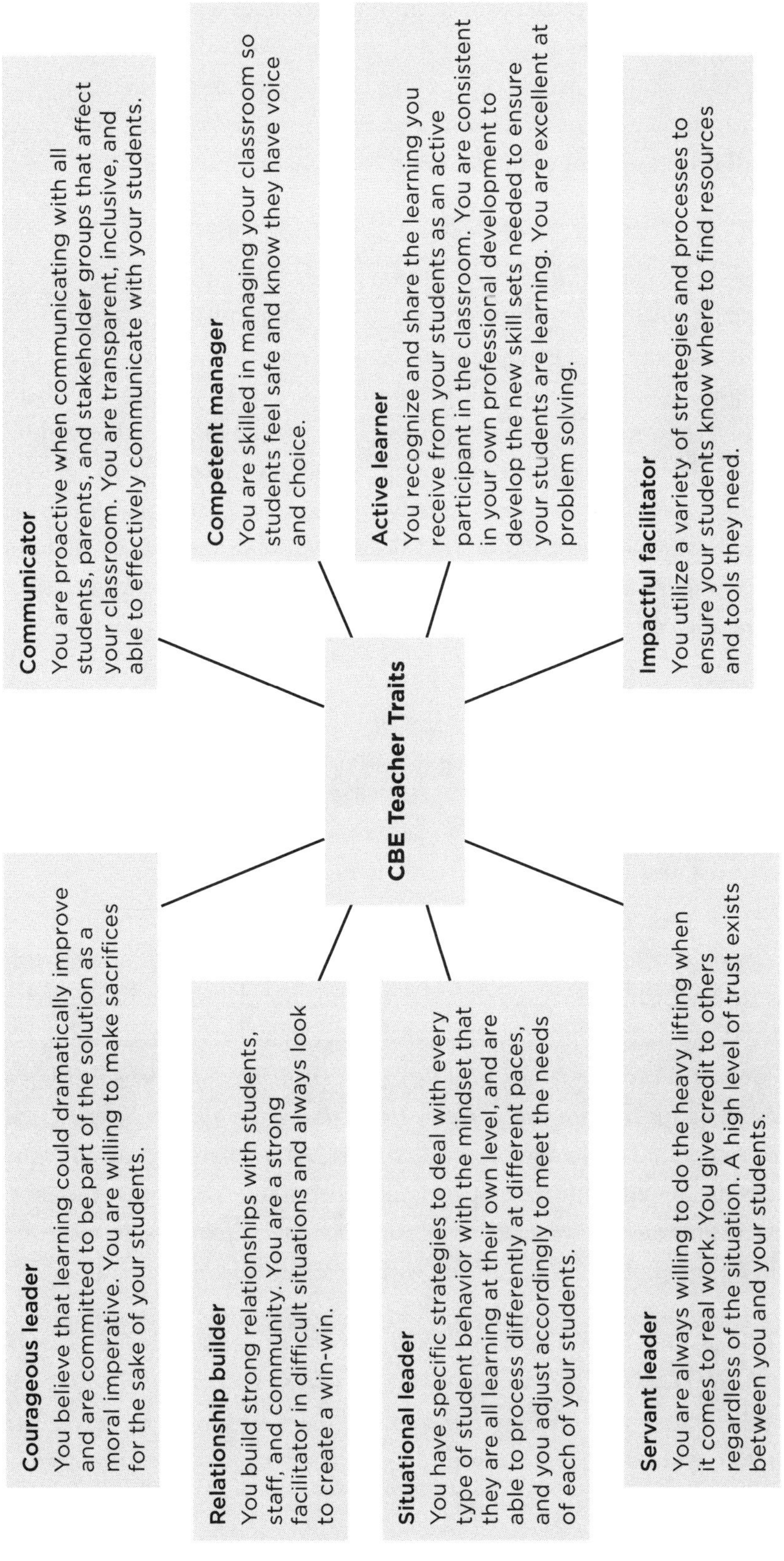

Figure 4.1: Key skill set of successful CBE teachers.

For Teachers, How Does the CBE System Compare to Traditional Systems?

CBE is an approach that works at all levels, for all students. CBE replaces traditional methods of hoping our students learn with intentional tools and processes to ensure that they learn, making adjustments along the way. To fully embrace CBE, teachers should have support from their principal and superintendent as well as policymakers, families, and especially the students. When leaders are reluctant to implement schoolwide or districtwide commitment to change to a CBE system, they can begin with a small number of individual teachers to flip their classrooms from traditional to mastery learning, which will see some success as the district decides if these pilot classrooms are really making a difference. The CBE approach works well with whole systems to ensure long-term impact, but it will also assist passionate individuals who have the courage to do what is best for their students.

When you walk through a CBE classroom, you immediately observe some differences in the way students and teachers are interacting with each other. You see teachers who may be giving some limited direct instruction; most of the time the teachers are interacting with small groups or individual students to assist them in their work to help provide direction for the next step. The direct instruction that does take place is often in the form of frontloading assignments. When frontloading assignments, teachers provide the majority of the necessary facts at the beginning of a unit or lesson so students then have what they need to dig deeper into specific topics and areas. For example, when students are learning the mathematical times tables, once they have memorized the tables, students can use that information to begin theorizing on rational numbers, infinity, and types of patterns. Another example might be teaching a broad topic such as war. A teacher might provide some facts about specific wars, how they were fought, and the outcomes; after frontloading the information, teachers release students to dive into reasons for conflict and resolutions that create a better world.

Even during the frontload of information, master teachers in traditional systems rarely stand and lecture for more than five to ten minutes. Through a variety of strategies, student groups can discover information in engaging ways. Most traditional teachers are familiar with Madelyn Hunter's (2004) six-step lesson plan and how important it is to provide anticipation for what will be the topic of learning, and guided instruction before launching students on their own to do the work. This is the same for the CBE system, but the difference is the transparency of what is going on, so students also have a voice in what and how they are learning. Example lesson templates are available at https://bit.ly/46Tt8yA for download. With AI, there are amazing tools at your fingertips, even for creating CBE lessons. The tools at

MagicSchool (https://magicschool.ai) are a great example that is free for teachers. The objectives may be the same, but the outcome is vastly different because students are now moving at their own pace, going slower when needed or speeding up when they are ready, without waiting for the rest of the class to catch up. This works well in any age classroom, from preschool through high school. Students who are too young to read yet use symbols, pictures, and graphics to see what is expected.

As a teacher, you will recognize the visuals around the CBE classroom that show targets for learning, resources, timelines, and how to get help when needed. Students can assess and learn from their mistakes from themselves, peers, the teacher, or even content experts. We often refer to them as business partners—people in the field who are partnering with the school to ensure students have real-life projects that help their community. T3 Alliance (https://t3alliance.org) has some great examples of community projects. Using the Stanford design thinking process, students learn to manage community projects starting with listening to what the real problem is. This skill is rarely taught, and most groups tend to want to jump to solutions before hearing the full story (Hasso Plattner Institute of Design at Stanford, 2012). The design thinking process consists of five stages: (1) empathize, (2) define, (3) ideate, (4) prototype, and (5) test. Ideate, prototype, and test work as a continual cycle; once one has moved into the test stage, they return to ideate (Hasso Plattner Institute of Design at Stanford, 2012).

As educators, the more "real" you make the lesson, the more enthusiastic students will become. When they realize that the project they are working on can actually help others and make a difference, their engagement increases a hundredfold. As overwhelming as it may seem to make business partners, think about how your students have access to unlimited resources through their relationships. Stanford's design thinking process has been a great help for many of the student groups we work with. This process shows each step and helps students learn basics of listening to what issues exist in the community.

Figure 4.2 briefly describes the steps of gaining business partners. Like any relationship, trust must be built based on common beliefs, and there needs to be something beneficial for all parties. It helps to have an introduction by someone you know.

Teachers today are expected to implement what they learned in college and practicum into day-to-day practice. However, colleges, universities, and teacher preparation programs struggle to keep up with the latest research and best practices. In a traditional system, teachers plan out their year in time increments, according to quarters and semesters, with measured learning that fits students within specific groups. CBE systems allow for identified competencies that are personalized for each student, now possible through technology tools. Different from tracking, the CBE system allows teachers to use data to drive their instruction, assessment, and

How to Find the Right Business Partner

Network
Use your parents, board, neighbors, civic groups, and others to introduce you to local businesses. Just knowing others helps when opportunities come for student projects. Even in grocery lines you can make connections by sharing your passion.

Define Values
To find a business partner, you must clearly define the purpose and qualities you want in a partner. It's important that the business values align with what you want learners to identify with.

Create a Win-Win
Most businesses are approached to give money or products. Create a relationship where both parties can help solve a community issue together. (Be sure to do background checks.)

Involve Student Leaders
Allow your leaders to help make connections of what they have to offer to help the business with an issue in the community. The project management needs a process like design thinking.

Create Solutions
Student leaders report to the business partner for clarification, ideas, prototypes, and solutions.

Figure 4.2: Finding business partners.

reporting. Teachers in traditional systems may be master teachers and able to make a difference in their students' lives, but they will always be limited in how effective they are only because of the system they are in.

One way to work in some CBE practices within the traditional system is for teachers to flip their classroom, which, as discussed in chapter 3 (page 41), means they can deliver some information remotely using technology in order to make better use of time in the classroom (Bergmann, 2022). This approach shows teachers how to go a step further for mastery learning to happen. Bergmann (2022) recognizes that this approach is better than most, but it still lacks the support of whole-system change. With CBE systems, teachers are supported throughout their school and district and have resources that are only available through the support of their leadership.

Following are some examples of the differences among traditional classrooms, flipped classrooms, and CBE classrooms. These examples chart the progression from a traditional classroom (block 1) to the introduction of a CBE system (block 2), the implementation of a CBE system with guided coaches gradually releasing control as the teacher gains skills and confidence (block 3), and finally the routine phase (block 4), where processes are in place to continually improve and learn from what we are doing to make it even better, ideally with colleagues also in the CBE system. The following figures give examples of what teachers might hear for feedback when the principal or a colleague walks through the classroom or takes time to do a classroom observation with the intention of helping improve the system. Figure 4.3 highlights observation.

Many awesome teachers would like to meet the needs of all their students, but most traditional systems demand following timelines that make it impossible to ensure quality for every student. Even with additional aides and support, the traditional system of teaching prepares students for jobs that will no longer exist by the time they graduate. Flipped classrooms give the teachers more time to interact with

Traditional	Flipped Class	CBE Start	CBE Refined
• Good traditional teaching (five-step lesson plan) • Shared vision • Code of collaboration • Standard operating procedures; tools and processes • Unpacking the learning and making this visible on the walls (scales written in students' terminology, rubrics, and so on)	• Voice and choice in simple ways • Classroom differentiation from direct instruction with learning stations or other choices • Data-driven decisions • Goal setting • Introduce the digital platform	• Monitoring the vision and code • Digital platform in practice with playlist • Gradual release of control from teacher directed to student directed • Acceleration of learning • Cool projects	• Refining all the processes • Students take more ownership of their learning • Students create their own playlist • Students create their own schedule • Results are accelerated (three years' growth in one year's time)

Figure 4.3: CBE progression on observation—Teacher view.

their students and transition to facilitating the class and allowing students to be curious and explore learning more. CBE systems provide voice and choice for students so they may have a say in what and how they learn while being guided by their teacher as a facilitator in partnership with them. Figure 4.4 shows the progression of the teacher's role.

Traditional grading systems are in place because it was the best way, when our education system started, to show some type of score to parents on how their child was progressing. However, this system doesn't show what they learned or how they are progressing or lacking in skills. It's what everyone knows and is familiar with, so the tradition continues. Flipped classrooms also use traditional grading but are able to move toward mastery rather than just a set grade with everyone moving together. Moving away from time-bound traditional systems, CBE students are given feedback to improve and keep on the journey toward mastery and eventually are able to get feedback from their peers and self-reflect to see what they need to improve on. Figure 4.5 (page 82) explores differences related to grading.

Another major difference among traditional, flipped, and CBE classrooms is curriculum and assessment. Master teachers in traditional systems go beyond the

Traditional	Flipped Class	CBE Start	CBE Refined
• Tight timelines to ensure all content is covered in a year; specialist assistance with students who need extra help or need more challenging gifted programs • Expectation that teachers are masters of all content presented	• More teacher availability during the school day since the direct instruction is now delivered via technology • Teacher facilitation in the room for hands-on, engaging projects	• Shift in teacher's role from a traditional one to that of a facilitator • Teacher adoption of an agile approach in which they constantly adjust their strategies to meet the needs of every student using a combination of whole-group, small-group, and individual instruction	• Teacher understanding of the art and science of the profession with students as partners • A new learning environment in which teachers are learners together with students regarding how to best meet their needs

Figure 4.4: CBE progression on teacher role—Teacher view.

Traditional	Flipped Class	CBE Start	CBE Refined
• A–F scoring based on specific time-bound measures • Example: Final quarter grades may be based on various combinations of participation, attendance, and test scores	• A–F scoring with some flexibility for measuring activities within the classroom, since there is more hands-on time	• Grading based on mastering personalized targets • Students may move forward when they are ready • Grades assigned when mastered and available 24/7 with the online platform	• Creates transparent and consistent expectations across classrooms for students, parents, teachers, and administrators • Dramatic increase of reliability and validity of this system

Figure 4.5: CBE progression on grading—Teacher view.

teacher textbook and utilize resources found in many areas. The curriculum is still governed by the district, and pacing depends on what the district has determined is age-appropriate, rather than individualized or personalized. With flipped classrooms, the instruction can be much more engaging and hands-on, with teachers giving their students more time and attention. The CBE system is set up to allow teachers a variety of resources and technologies to manage diversity and choice while ensuring quality learning (see figure 4.6).

The last major difference is instruction. Many master teachers in traditional systems have found the balanced instructional model to provide some direct instruction, some group work, and some individual time to work. In flipped classrooms, students learn from other resources the teacher provides outside of class so the time in class for instruction can be much deeper and more engaging. In CBE instruction, students are partners in their learning and get some choice on methods and projects that they are passionate about to show their mastery of learning. Figure 4.7 provides a summary of the progression in instruction.

Traditional	Flipped Class	CBE Start	CBE Refined
• Traditional core subjects plus some electives • Mostly textbook driven with pencil-and-paper testing A–F scoring based on specific time-bound measures	• Traditional core subjects with some flexibility for delivery systems • More authentic assessments with students demonstrating mastery learning	• Reprioritization of what students need to know, be able to do, and be like, and a stronger emphasis on integrating 21st century skills • Performance tasks and projects driven by clear scales	• Students create multidisciplinary projects that solve real-world problems, thus increasing student engagement and preparing them for their future

Figure 4.6: CBE progression on curriculum and assessment—Teacher view.

Traditional	Flipped Class	CBE Start	CBE Refined
• One size fits all; students move on even if they are not ready for next steps • Whole-group instruction dominates the delivery system • Prescribed programs and textbooks drive instruction	• Instruction is "flipped" to be available as homework; class time is hands-on, with engaging projects demonstrating the learning	• Balanced instruction (students must first understand then apply in real-life situations or hands-on projects) • Differentiated instruction, thus meeting individual students at the point of their needs and interests • Instruction given in class, at home, and in the world, balancing resources and opportunities	• Meets needs of all students, resulting in more efficient and effective learning • Increase in equity • Instruction that is not just about learning skills but about applying them in a meaningful way, thereby increasing student engagement

Figure 4.7: CBE progression on instruction—Teacher view.

What Do Primary and Secondary Teacher Perspectives Look Like in CBE?

This section features specific examples that classroom teachers might find useful. Following is a day in the life of a teacher that might help visualize what it would be like to teach in a CBE system. This story, fictional but based on Roxanne's experience, provides a glimpse of what it looks like to teach in a CBE system.

> *Looking around her classroom, Char looked with satisfaction at the classroom layout. This year would be different for her. Coming into her preK–2 classroom, students could see where their personal spots were organized to independently put away their coats and backpacks and change their shoes. The learning stations were set up for the first few weeks of school where students would choose one as they waited for others to arrive and the teacher to formally begin the day. They could see the chart where they would build their classroom collaboration tools to ensure everyone knew what was expected of them; they could assess it throughout the day and reflect on it each afternoon.*
>
> *Char knew her parents had high expectations, believing their children had potential to become leaders in their community. She wanted to extend that belief to the learning environment. Students could see they were safe to explore new ideas and create failures in their growth of learning how to solve problems. Throughout the day, she had planned time to allow for group discussions and reflections so each student could learn from the others and know that all perspectives would be respected.*
>
> *As the students arrived, she was pleased to see their enthusiasm for their new space. Throughout the day, they were allowed time to choose specific tasks and see what they already knew to be able to move on toward their learning goals. Some of her students had lots of support already and were reading, but most still needed to begin with phonics and the alphabet. She knew from her experience of setting up the culture of the classroom that the older students would step into the role of mentoring the younger students. This allowed them to strengthen their skills as she observed and supervised them. Char had planned her units as overall themes: first outdoors, taking advantage of the warm fall weather and allowing the students some wiggle time in the fresh air. Outside, she watched them group around a butterfly. As she praised them for noticing, she used the teachable moment to have the students describe what they were seeing and why. The wonder of the perfect symmetry of the butterfly was inspiring for the art later, but it also opened the discussion toward the life of a butterfly and how it changes. Her students all contributed to what they knew*

about change in their own life and how scary it can be, especially starting a new school year.

Char knew these discussions and time together with informal talks helped build relationships and trust so her students knew she cared. It allowed for establishing rules of what the class could expect within the time they were together. She was pleased to see their chart at the end of the day, with the rules they came up with that included respect, kindness, one person talking at a time, and raising their hands. You could already feel the calmness settling in as they reflected as a class, moving the arrow right or left and assessing their behaviors together. This tool was just one of hundreds her mentor was sharing and helping her master, just like she did for her own students. CBE spans across her classroom, her school, and her own professional life, allowing her to feel supported and balanced with her life outside of school.

The following narrative is a composite of many experiences of a secondary teacher in a CBE system. Teachers are highly qualified in specific subjects but collaborate across content areas to provide learning opportunities that are unique for the students' needs. Ella would traditionally be a tenth-grade social studies teacher with a minor in language arts.

Looking around her classroom, Ella observed students helping other students in small groups they had formed to collaborate on their projects addressing specific standards, not only in her world history classroom but also in the language arts classroom of her colleague next door. Some students were working alone, and others were waiting for more advice on how they might proceed. Ella was helping the students be successful at setting their daily goals so they had confidence to establish good habits for their learning routines. She realized that a year ago, she also struggled with setting goals, but CBE helped her see the value of setting small goals to get started, and then gradually increasing the complexity of her goals to help her plan ahead with intentional outcomes. It wasn't always easy without the traditional textbook type of learning. She can remember the confidence she felt in following the teacher's manual, page by page, each day. It was nice to have all the answers. But looking around the classroom, Ella saw that her students were so much more engaged than they had been previously, being allowed choice in how they learned within the guidelines they set together as a class.

Almost a month into the school year, Ella saw the omnivore students, who would do well in any system, excelled in the competency-based district where they could move at their own pace and help others along the way. Students who generally struggled to grasp certain concepts also excelled, as they were able to use their strengths in other areas, so each student recognized how unique they were and how they could help each other by working together. Ella had never worked in an environment where everyone was truly collaborative rather than competitive. The first two weeks of school were chaotic, as each teacher team helped facilitate groups of students solidifying what they felt their school should look like, feel like, sound like, and act like. The rotation between the social-emotional topics and the academics was a seamless transition to prepare students for success. This investment of time first thing in the school year provided clear expectations that were consistent throughout the school and district.

Ella got a ping on her laptop as she was finishing her last group. It reminded her of Billy's mastering a competency standard and looking for feedback. As she opened the student management system, she saw Billy's evidence of how and why he had mastered it. She could easily share he was proficient and would move on, but she knew this lesson was fairly easy for Billy, and she sent him a note back with the proficient grade, but also a challenge for him to take it just a bit further by teaching it to someone who had not mastered it yet and become advanced. It would cause him to be a bit uncomfortable, but she knew he was ready for it, and it helped Billy learn a bit deeper.

The five students came to her class at the weekly designated time for CORE Court, their student-created discipline process. Ella had volunteered as the teacher this week to help lend credibility to the process by overseeing the proceedings. The student leaders had all gone through the training process and now had an opportunity to demonstrate the personal social skills they had mastered to help other students learn from mistakes and try new strategies for self-correcting and keeping the school moving in a positive direction.

Preparing her lessons in three-week units helped Ella organize her themes for the year, planning with the end in mind. This ensured the students would get through a set of competencies in an average pacing, knowing they could also move ahead with their own ILP they developed with their teachers, and provided more time for others who might need a bit longer to understand the concepts. Grading had become much easier with the new system, since all the competencies were transparent for teachers, administrators, parents, and especially the students. It was a joy to see the students be empowered for their own learning. Ella couldn't remember how many times, even in this past month, students had asked if they could stay longer because they hadn't quite finished their project. Ella had never worked in a school where students were having so much fun they didn't want to leave. With the digital platform available 24/7, pacing, feedback, grading, and reporting were ongoing, so there was no huge buildup of grades that caused her to stay late nights, like in her other teaching jobs. Her family appreciated how much she was present when at home instead of being so run down and out of energy from the day job. This type of teaching still required a lot of time and energy, but it was so much more efficient for her time management and personal life. It also made it easier for those tough conversations when students were not meeting their expected pacing. Ella had a positive rapport to communicate as a team working together for each student's success.

Working within a CBE system, students' voices and choices should be heard from the incubation period, and then carried on throughout the changes and adjustments. Students who are able to see what they need to know gain confidence in their abilities and feel safe to try the next lesson. The following are tools teachers can use to guide and assess students on their individualized projects. Two ways we highlight here are (1) ILPs and (2) playlists or lesson plans.

Individual Learning Plans

As students start asking for special projects based on their passions, one way they are able to show mastery of learning targets and work in teams is through an ILP. This tool is most appropriate for secondary students; elementary students can use playlists (see next section, page 94). They can create their own ILP that shows what targets they are addressing, how they plan to do the work, how they will demonstrate mastery, and what permissions they require. All the ILPs we have used include a place to receive a teacher endorsement for their idea. Most ILPs last five to ten days.

For example, one of our students started a job shadow because he decided he wanted to explore what it would be like to be a chef in one of the top restaurants in Anchorage. We happened to have a substitute teacher in the room next door who worked there part-time, and she knew the head chef. She called him on her break, and he agreed to have the young man come, but only if he could recruit four others to make five total so his time would be worth it. The young man quickly recruited four others who got the ILP completed and went off to the restaurant the next week. One of the friends, who was a robotics captain, ended up majoring in culinary arts and eventually opening an Italian restaurant after studying in Italy later. He had not even considered cooking before that experience, and now his life had taken a turn all due to the opportunity that happened as a result of students having some voice and choice. Following is an example of the ILP (figure 4.8, page 88) they used, which clearly lists the standards they used as learning targets and includes a rubric that made expectations for each level of performance clear. Roxanne recalls the joy with which they returned together to class, all excited about what they had just learned.

Individual Learning Plan

Student Name: ______________ **Date:** ________ **Advisor:** ______________

Project Title: ____________ **Job Shadow (place):** ____________ **Due:** ________

Learning Targets:

CC.LT 2.01	Shows understanding, friendliness, and respect for feelings of others; asserts oneself when appropriate; takes an interest in what people say and why they think and act as they do.
CC.LT 2.06	Identifies skills for safety in a variety of work (school) settings. (Includes appropriate dress and behavior for activity/environment.)
CC.LT 2.09	Identifies several possible careers and practices interview procedures with one business/community partner.
CC.LT 2.10	Identifies and explains five postsecondary pathways (vocational training, college/university, entrepreneurial endeavors, military or directly to work) and practices preemployment skills (proper phone etiquette, eye contact, handshakes, and so on).
CC.LT 3.03	Arrives at school and/or work site and performs scheduled activities on time.
CC.LT 3.07	Completes a job shadow or site visit to a business and posts summary on web Life Skills Portfolio.
SL.SC 2.01	Employs effective group interaction skills (taking turns, coming to consensus, sharing, accepting ideas, communicating positively and constructively, and so on).
CC.LT 2.07	Collects and organizes relevant information for web-based Life Skills Portfolio (including résumé and recommendation letters, awards, certificates, and so on).
TL.CA 1.01	Uses word processing tools (dictionary, thesaurus, grammar check, word count, and so on) to perform simple editing tasks (for example, checking for spelling, punctuation, capitalization).
TL.CA 1.02	Uses proper keyboarding position (body posture, eye level, and so on) when working on computers (ergonomics).
TL.CA 1.03	Identifies and uses appropriate software for tasks with guidance.
TL.CA 2.03	Accesses educational resources on the internet.

Plan: Confirm with business date and time for job shadow. Look up information on Alaska's AKCIS website about what people are required to have for education and training in this field. Look up two alternative jobs in a similar field. Prepare interview questions. Arrange for a ride. Get ILP signed by all teachers, parent, advisor, and principal. Dress correctly and be there a few minutes early. Shadow the business-person. Take notes. Take pictures. Get business card. Write a thank-you letter. Write reflection. Meet with your teacher for final assessment.

Possible challenges: Confirming time and date. Speaking up. Doing the research and preparation before my job shadow. Completing thank-you letter and reflection within a week of doing your job shadow.

Student Signature: ____________ **Parent Signature:** ____________

Teacher Signature: ____________ **Advisor Signature:** ____________

Out-of-School ILP: ____________

Employer or Organization: ____________

Location or Address: ____________ **Phone:** ____________

Principal's Signature: ____________ **Effective Dates:** ____________

Attach Job-Shadow Worksheet to ILP

Job-Shadow or Career Exploration Scoring Guide: ____________

Career development (target: CC.LT 3.07—Completes a job shadow or site visit to a business and posts summary on web Life Skills Portfolio.)

	Advanced	**Proficient**	**Developing**	**Emerging**
Prior to the Experience (Preparation)	• Articulately, confidently, and positively states purpose and expectations of the job-shadow experience • Seeks additional information on-site by researching and/or asking in-depth questions prior to experience	• Understands purpose and value of job shadow and can convey to others • Prepares three questions ready to ask at site • Has materials and is prompt (pen, paper, questions, and so on) • Obtains all necessary information	• Understands at least one purpose of job shadow • Needs assistance from facilitator to think of three questions to ask the job-shadow host • Is on time most of the time and is prepared with most of the necessary materials	• Does not listen to introductory information and requirements • Does not prepare questions for site host • Does not have necessary materials and is late

Figure 4.8: Project ILP—Job-shadow example.

continued →

	Advanced	Proficient	Developing	Emerging
During the Experience (Job Shadow or Career Exploration)	• Requests to be more involved (hands-on work) and shows capability to do this • Takes notes that include impressions and facts • Asks all prepared questions articulately and with interest, expanding when appropriate • Displays exemplary pre-employment and interpersonal skills	• Introduces self upon meeting host • Asks thoughtful, relevant questions and is actively involved during the visit • Dress, manners, and attitude reflect positively on student and program • Records factual notes • Conveys interest in site (eye contact, smile, affirmations, respectful comments, and so on)	• Is hesitant with introductions—waits until the host introduces first • Uses inconsistent eye contact with the host or lack of interest • Shows willing interest and participates in conversation some of the time • Asks questions that are unclear or have already been answered in conversation	• Displays lack of respect for the presenter (not paying attention, putting others down, fidgeting, laughing, and so on) or lacks enthusiasm • Does not participate in discussions or ask questions • Gives little or no response to host's questions • Dresses inappropriately
After the Experience (Reflection)	• Reflects on what was learned, relevance to life, possible further exploration, and so on • Writes, checks, revises, and sends a grammatically correct and articulate thank-you letter with personal specifics	• Completes required reflection in a quality manner • Reflection conveys to others what student learned • Writes, requests editing on, revises, and sends a professional thank-you letter	• Attempts to share what student learned, but lacks clarity or a relevant connection to student's own life • Some effort is put forth, but does not or cannot write a professional thank-you letter	• Refuses to complete reflection or share it with others or does not understand the reflection process • Does not create an effective thank-you letter

Please post any comments on the back. Thank you for helping with this experience!

Any questions? Please contact ________________________.

Source for standards: Alaska Department of Education and Early Development, n.d.

Following are a few additional examples of other projects students in CBE systems have done.

Students from several adjoining districts came together in the summer of 2013 in Denali National Park in Alaska to learn about hands-on science and storytelling. They worked with the park service to create photos and a curriculum that would help other students appreciate what they could learn in the park. They were able to set up satellite relays that allowed them to extend internet access over an area of the park. This meant they could communicate with experts in the field as well as others around the park, including tourists who were not able to enter the park due to conditions such as fires or overcrowding. Through conferencing in the field, they coordinated hooking up sensors to locate wolves and monitor their dens for activity, allowing them to learn more about the park's wolf population. Another group of students was monitoring the firefighters and learning what happens to the flora and fauna after a fire.

The difference we saw with these projects compared to traditional student projects is that the students received tools and opportunities, and then they felt confident to explore the science behind their interests, work collaboratively with the business partners and each other, and really make a difference. These projects were much more extreme than most programs could manage, but the ideas are transferable, to use technology to inspire students to interact with nature in real ways that make differences with their communities. You can read more about our hands-on STEAM (science, technology, engineering, arts and culture, and mathematics) activities that we have carried on through the T3 Alliance (www.t3alliance.org). The assessment rubric in figure 4.9 (page 92) is adapted from the national technology standards (International Society for Technology in Education [ISTE], 1998). The school created the rubric based on the national standards so it could assess students from a variety of districts.

All work is tied to competencies (formerly national standards) that have rubrics or scales to explain expectations. This allows students, families, and all stakeholders to see what is expected without trying to second-guess the teacher for an A grade.

Another example from Roxanne's experience is when several students approached the school with a project they wanted to do with the school district offices that were in the building next to the school. They created a public service announcement (PSA) because the slippery ice was causing people to get hurt outside the school. The students noticed this and wanted to do something besides just spreading sand, so they asked if the district would like a PSA. These three students went on to lead a class for video editing. They were excited to take what they learned and

Learning Target	Advanced	Proficient	Developing	Emerging
Students Standard 5.b **Exhibit a positive attitude toward using technology that supports collaboration, learning, and productivity.**	• Consistently and actively advocates a positive attitude toward using technology that supports collaboration, learning, and productivity • Consistently practices a positive attitude toward using technology that supports collaboration, learning, and productivity	• Exhibits a positive attitude toward using technology that supports collaboration, learning, and productivity	• Sometimes exhibits a positive attitude toward using technology that supports collaboration, learning, and productivity	• Is aware of the need to have a positive attitude toward using technology that supports collaboration, learning, and productivity

Source for standard: ISTE, 1998. Used with permission.

Figure 4.9: Proficiency scale for a technology standard.

help other students. The following chart (figure 4.10) shows an example of a rubric created for the students doing this technology project.

Students love it when they are the expert at something. As we give them voice and choice, they come up with amazing ways to show us mastery. When Roxanne was at the Alaska Department of Education and Early Development, some of the students from Lower Kuskokwim School District (Mountain Village, Alaska) came online through videoconference with her because they wanted to demonstrate mastery of their learning. Their facilitator in the room had shown them how to use their SMART Board to work through mathematics problems together. As a fourth-grade student stood up, his grandpa was there, as many elders support their community and school, and he walked through the process by standing to the side and allowing his grandpa to do the SMART Board and question. The image of the young teaching the old was priceless, and the commissioner who was also present understood the power of the processes and tools we were talking about in CBE.

Learning Target: TL.CA 4.03—Develops, publishes, and presents technology-based multimedia products (such as a webpage with graphics, links, and so on) using technology that demonstrates and communicates curriculum concepts inside or outside the classroom.

	Advanced	Proficient	Developing	Emerging
Multimedia Software	Independently design, develop, and publish three or more products tied to curriculum using advanced features of technology software and hardware, and teaches others how to do so.	Independently designs, develops, and publishes three or more products tied to curriculum using advanced features of technology software and hardware (for example, a presentation using such features as timers, transitions, movies, sounds, pictures, macros, video, text, and so on). Presents at least one product to an audience.	Designs, develops, and publishes at least two products tied to curriculum using advanced features of technology software and hardware with some help. Presents at least one product to an audience.	Designs and develops at least one product tied to curriculum using some features of technology software and hardware with great help.

Source for standard: Alaska Department of Education and Early Development, n.d.

Figure 4.10: Proficiency scale for a multimedia technology standard.

Over the years, the way we have been making incremental changes toward CBE is through the T3 Alliance, which allowed us to get funding through the National Science Foundation to help after-school programs learn STEM (science, technology, engineering, and mathematics) as we integrated growth mindset and community projects. One program in Hawaii used what they had learned with the Raspberry Pi technology to build computers and integrate air sensors. When the volcanoes erupted locally on the Big Island of Hawaii, families were evacuating quickly, and then the wind would shift and the air quality would change. Students set up air quality sensor monitors using the Raspberry Pis and worked with the emergency broadcasts to give real-time information on the air. They made national news, and the students could see how their work affected their communities (Low, 2020).

Lesson Plans and Playlists

Any teacher will appreciate the necessity of creating quality lesson plans. In a CBE classroom, we call lesson plans *playlists*—menus of options for fulfilling the requirements of the assigned learning. There are many resources available to find out more about playlists, including Marzano's High Reliability Schools Toolkit (www.marzanoresources.com). Other online resources are also available at little or no cost to teachers—for example, Open Educational Resources (https://oercommons.org); Jonathan Eckert's (2021) *Edutopia* article "10 Teacher Picks for Best Tech Tools"; and the George Lucas Educational Foundation, which publishes the *Edutopia* website. The need for a good plan is there no matter what system you are teaching in. The difference between CBE and traditional systems is that learners are moving at their own pace and not everyone in the class will be working on the same project at the same time. Their selection of projects will depend on individual students' readiness and prerequisite knowledge to be there. This is where technology is vital. A CBE digital platform is the only way to successfully implement this type of personalized learning without burning out the teachers, ideally with an AI component to help on the journey of creating personalized playlists or lesson plans. We have done this using traditional learning management systems and even by hand (Excel spreadsheets, teacher workbooks, and so on), but the work involved is not sustainable. As a teacher, you will need to decide if your district is ready with the supporting tools. If not, you may want to engage in an individual teacher or pilot program with a small cohort to implement a portion as proof of concept. There are many different levels of support to implement CBE, just like you would do in your classroom for different levels of readiness in students.

A sample playlist for elementary students will look simpler, but it still has the main elements of voice and choice for the learners. For example, a teacher may have a unit focusing on alternative energy. For elementary, students might select a playlist that gives four choices: (1) station in the room that provides hands-on testing for how electricity works (simple circuit board), (2) wheel to blow to demonstrate how wind turbines work, (3) water dropping from a distance to see the power of moving an object, and (4) biomass to learn how photosynthesis changes the sun's energy into oxygen through plants. Depending on the level of the student, there could be challenges to draw, paint, or color alternative energies they can dream up. Or they could create a story of how energy saved a town. Figure 4.11 provides a sample playlist for a unit on sources of energy.

Following is an example of a secondary playlist in a CBE system (figure 4.12, page 96). (See page 111 for a blank reproducible version of this figure.)

Ms. Roxy's Class
Energy Playlist

Choose from one of the following:

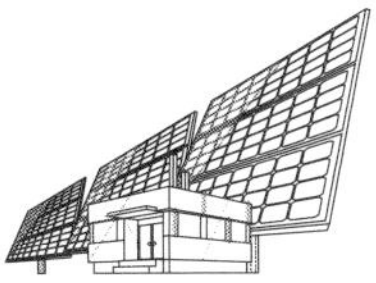
1. Solar Power

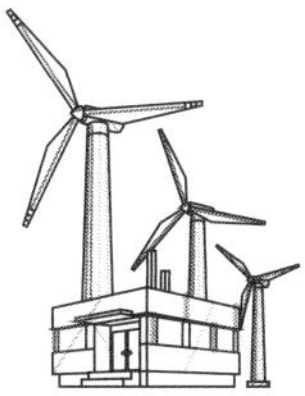
2. Wind Power

3. Hydro Power

4. Biomass Power

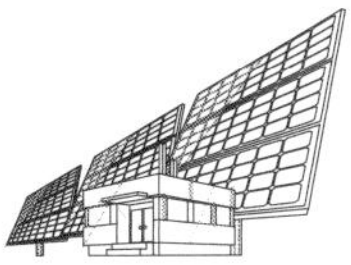

Solar Power

Check out how the sun can give energy to make things move! Choose one item to put into the sunlight and see what happens. Share what you discovered with a partner. Why do you think this happened? What else could you use solar power for?

Wind Power

Check out how the wind can give energy to make energy! See what happens when the wind comes on. Share what you discovered with a partner. Why do you think this happened? What else could you use wind power for?

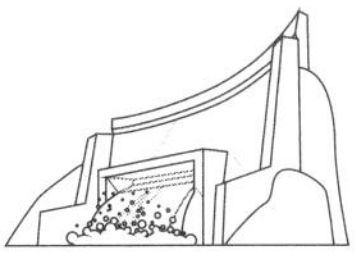

Hydro Power

Create a monitor for hydro power, using the Raspberry Pi to measure flow as small as a garden hose, to discover ways to conserve and use the smallest of resources. The flow of water powers the bank of batteries to power greenhouses and other small, energy-efficient projects.

Biomass Power

Check out how the plants transform energy from the sun to oxygen in the air! Draw out what you see happening in the plant cycle. Learn the song.

My Reflection

Name: ____ Date: ______________

Which one did I do?

What happened?

How might other things be powered from this?

Figure 4.11: Sample playlist for an elementary classroom.

<table>
<tr><th colspan="5">Title: My Alaskan Community: Elfin Cove</th></tr>
<tr><td colspan="2">Grade Level: 10</td><td colspan="3">Content Area: Alaska Studies</td></tr>
<tr><td colspan="5">Overview:
After the overview of the geography of Alaska, students will do a deep dive into a specific community.</td></tr>
<tr><td colspan="5">Learning Targets</td></tr>
<tr><td>SE.AN 4.04</td><td colspan="4">Explains how societies' values may affect an individual's point of view and interpretation of facts.</td></tr>
<tr><td colspan="5">Cross-Curricular Connection
Language Arts—Communication Literacy</td></tr>
<tr><td>CL.WP.06.01</td><td colspan="4">Ideas: Samples are based on complex themes or theses, which are supported throughout the work.</td></tr>
<tr><td>CL.WP.06.02</td><td colspan="4">Organization: Writes well-organized papers in the correct format for the writing situation.</td></tr>
<tr><td colspan="5">Assessments (see student handout)</td></tr>
<tr><td>Target</td><td>Advanced</td><td>Proficient</td><td>Developing</td><td>Emerging</td></tr>
<tr><td>CL.WP.06.01.01
Ideas</td><td>• Theme is developed throughout the piece.
• Information makes the reader want to keep reading more.
• Creative approach is maintained throughout the piece.
• Title captures reader's attention with creativity and appeal.</td><td>• Compositions are based on complex themes.
• Relevant, telling, and quality details give important information that goes beyond the obvious or predictable.
• Attempts a creative approach or form; ideas are fresh and original.
• Title is original and captures the central theme of the piece.</td><td>• Attempts to build a complex theme.
• Sometimes details are relevant, telling, and of quality; attempts to give important information that goes beyond the obvious or predictable.
• Sometimes creative or fresh and original.
• Title is there and addresses the topic appropriately.</td><td>• A theme exists and is maintained.
• Details give information on the topic, but may be simplistic.
• Ideas relate to the thesis.
• Title is there, but simplistic.</td></tr>
<tr><td>CL.WP.06.02.01
Organization</td><td>• Introduction presents a creative and expressive thesis statement that is manageable.
• Includes well-developed body paragraphs with researched examples that consistently prove the thesis and force the reader to think about the issue.</td><td>• Introduction presents a clear thesis statement.</td><td>• Thesis may be too wordy or vague for writing a cohesive paper.</td><td>• Thesis is off or may be missing.
• Paragraphs may not support the thesis.</td></tr>
</table>

Target	Advanced	Proficient	Developing	Emerging
CL.WP.06.02.01 Organization (*Continued*)	• Transitions between paragraphs flow. • Conclusion teaches overall idea to audience, and motivates them for thinking and action on the topic presented.	• Includes well-developed body paragraphs with clear examples that consistently support the thesis and topic sentences for the given format. • Transitions between paragraphs are present and effective. • Conclusion teaches the overall idea to the audience.	• Few body paragraphs, or body paragraphs may need more development with stronger examples in order to consistently prove the thesis. • Transitions exist between some of the paragraphs. • Conclusion restates the thesis and summarizes key points.	• Attempts to use transitions. • Conclusion may be absent or unorganized.
SE.PR 4.04 Points of View **Explains how societies' values may affect an individual's point of view and interpretation of facts**	• Student identifies situations where societies' values have affected an individual's point of view and interpretation of facts. • Student analyzes characteristics of those societies that may have led to this effect on an individual's point of view. • Student explores outcomes of these scenarios in the historical context.	• Student identifies situations where societies' values have affected an individual's point of view and interpretation of facts. • Student analyzes characteristics of those societies that may have led to this effect on an individual's point of view.	• Student identifies situations where societies' values have affected an individual's point of view and interpretation of facts.	• Student identifies situations where societies' values have affected an individual's point of view.

Materials

You may find your information from first-person (primary) sources, from direct interviews, from websites, or in the news. Be sure to always cite your sources and check for accuracy and reliability.

Alaska History Course Online (Alaska Humanities Forum site; www.akhistorycourse.org)

Alaska Institute of the North (www.institutenorth.org)

Alaska Department of Education and Early Development (https://education.alaska.gov)

Alaska Department of Community and Regional Affairs Community Profiles (https://bit.ly/49yEHN7)

University of Alaska Anchorage LitSite: Alaska Kids (https://bit.ly/3wn98rb)

Figure 4.12: CBE lesson plan sample.

continued →

Anticipatory Set:

Begin with a Kahoot! fun quiz to see what students may already know. Allow for a fast-paced game followed by rich discussion for sharing stories about places in Alaska and personal experiences. Review primary and secondary sources and how to validate information.

Direct Instruction:

Allow students to interject personal experiences in each of the five regions presented, talking about what they saw and did, who they interacted with, and why they were there.

5 Regions of Alaska by Larry Csonka: https://youtu.be/1tvOSYmpUEO

Deep dive: Show two-minute video about a community (Elfin Cove) by Sixel Consulting Group: https://youtu.be/uAyqBSoKTQM

Modeling:

Students are grouped by counting off by fours. Each group takes one section to reflect on what they saw and what else they might include for location, description, industries, and demographics. Time them for two to three minutes (watching to see if they are engaged or finished and ready for the next step). Share out and have a class discussion about other things they might want to include. Then, as a whole class, brainstorm what was unique and why. This is the hardest part because it goes deep into not just what we are seeing at face value, but also the why behind what we are seeing because of the history, culture, and values that can only be found by talking with the people there. Lead the discussion toward how students might find this information in a respectful way (through interviewing real people) and the process for interviews, active listening, note taking, clarifying facts, follow-up, and so on.

Checking for Understanding:

Break into different groups to see how much students understand the expectations of the lesson moving forward (selecting their own community and how to get the information they will need).

Guided Practice:

Give students time to research a community they would like to explore more. Ask for volunteers to share a name of the community and then as a whole class brainstorm ways they might get the information they will need and also what issues they might run into to be sensitive about. Anticipate what some of the challenges might be and how to navigate conversations respectfully.

Closure:

Show video of a neighborhood in Anchorage, Alaska (the largest city in the state), and how this is so different from Elfin Cove (https://youtu.be/10HMnUhAEFQ). End with a discussion about the points of view and perspectives.

Independent Practice:

Direct students to come back for next class with a community selected and know some basic facts. We will work together as a class to provide feedback (using the critical friends peer review process) to help them consider what else to include and how they want to present their final products (story, news, video, podcast, and so on).

Attachments

My Alaska Community Profile

Critical Friends Peer Review Process

Alaska Storytelling With Interviews

Source for standards: Mourant, 2011.

The following playlist (figure 4.13) is part of the lesson on the community. This version is to provide an example of what teachers might produce for their own lessons. The assessment rubric was created for students who want to submit their project through a paper.

Title: My Alaskan Community				
Student Name or Names: ____				
Community Location: ____				
Community Description: ____				
Community Industries: ____				
Community Demographics: ____				
What we found unique about this community and why: Cite your sources.				
Assessments: When submitting work, score yourself and explain your reasoning.				
Learning Target	**Advanced**	**Proficient**	**Developing**	**Emerging**
SE.PR 4.04 Points of View Explains how societies' values may affect an individual's point of view and interpretation of facts	• Student identifies situations where societies' values have affected an individual's point of view and interpretation of facts. • Student analyzes characteristics of those societies that may have led to this effect on an individual's point of view. • Student explores outcomes of these scenarios in the historical context.	• Student identifies situations where societies' values have affected an individual's point of view and interpretation of facts. • Student analyzes characteristics of those societies that may have led to this effect on an individual's point of view.	• Student identifies situations where societies' values have affected an individual's point of view and interpretation of facts.	• Student identifies situations where societies' values have affected an individual's point of view.
CL.WP.06.01.01 Ideas	• Theme is developed throughout the piece. • Information makes reader want to keep reading more.	• Compositions are based on complex themes. • Relevant, telling, and quality details give important information that goes beyond the obvious or predictable.	• Attempts to build a complex theme. • Sometimes details are relevant, telling, and of quality; attempts to give important information that goes beyond the obvious or predictable.	• A theme exists and is maintained. • Details give information on the topic, but may be simplistic. • Ideas relate to thesis.

Figure 4.13: Lesson plan template with a proficiency scale for high school.

continued →

Learning Target	Advanced	Proficient	Developing	Emerging
CL.WP.06.01.01 Ideas (*Continued*)	• Creative approach is maintained throughout the piece. • Title captures reader's attention with creativity and appeal.	• Attempts a creative approach or form; ideas are fresh and original. • Title is original and captures the central theme of the piece.	• Sometimes creative or fresh and original. • Title is there and addresses the topic appropriately.	• Title is there, but simplistic.
CL.WP.06.02.01 Organization	• Introduction presents a creative and expressive thesis statement that is manageable. • Includes well-developed body paragraphs with researched examples that consistently prove the thesis and force the reader to think about the issue. • Transitions between paragraphs flow. • Conclusion teaches overall idea to audience and motivates them for thinking and action on the topic presented.	• Introduction presents a clear thesis statement. • Includes well-developed body paragraphs with clear examples that consistently support the thesis and topic sentences for the given format. • Transitions between paragraphs are present and effective. • Conclusion teaches the overall idea to the audience.	• Thesis may be too wordy or vague for writing a cohesive paper. • Few body paragraphs, or body paragraphs may need more development with stronger examples in order to consistently prove the thesis. • Transitions exist between some of the paragraphs. • Conclusion restates the thesis and summarizes key points.	• Thesis is off or may be missing. • Paragraphs may not support the thesis. • Attempts to use transitions. • Conclusion may be absent or unorganized.

Source for standards: Alaska Department of Education and Early Development, n.d.

What Does the Teacher Road Map to CBE Implementation Look Like?

Moving from traditional instruction to CBE can be daunting. Those who have gone before you have experiences and stories to help guide you through the steps. Following is a comprehensive road map, which provides a scope and sequence of events that are necessary to implement CBE at the classroom level; similar road maps do the same for leaders at the school level (chapter 5, page 113) and district level (chapter 6, page 139).

The road map helps teachers see the progression they must undertake to be successful. Every classroom will look different depending on its unique situation and readiness level. For a quick overview of the road map, refer back to figure 2.11 (page 33). The rest of this section explores each stage as it focuses on teachers.

After you have the information on what CBE is, you should begin with checking to see if you're really ready to embark on this journey. It's a long road, but well worth the effort when you see your students confident and enjoying learning. Many teachers are excellent traditional teachers and can make huge impacts on their students without CBE. However, if you really want to embrace current research that shows us CBE is superior to traditional systems (Marzano & Abbott, 2022; Marzano et al., 2022; Reigeluth & Karnopp, 2013), you have the power to make a change. It might begin with just flipping your classroom so learning during the school day becomes much more hands-on and engaging.

The first step toward CBE is understanding the difference between traditional systems and CBE. Reading this book should help you check that off the list. The second step toward CBE, readiness, sounds like this: *I must be ready for change and open to new ideas of what education looks like, feels like, and acts like.* You should consider the following questions.

- What isn't working in my class right now?
- Do my classes have wide gaps in ability and motivation?
- Is there a strategy that can address what is broken in my class?
- Do I have the strategies to meet the varied needs of my students?
- What do I know about CBE and traditional classrooms?
- What are my current strategies to support good teaching and learning?
- Do I have adequate strategies to meet the needs of my students?
- What are the differences between traditional teaching and CBE?
- Where are my gaps in implementing CBE?
- Where should I begin?

Your next steps, if you feel you are ready for this, include the following.

- Participate in CBE training.
- Complete a self-assessment on your readiness.
- Create a road map and prioritize steps to support CBE in your classroom.

Each of the steps involves the essential questions and resources to implement for success. In chapter 2 (page 17), we shared charts (starting with figure 2.2 on page 21) to show you some of the benefits, hopefully encouraging you to take those first steps in your journey. These provide specific examples of the benefits of engaging in this journey. It is not easy and will take time, but hopefully you are beginning to see the benefits, not the least of which is that it really is the best thing for your students.

There are six stages to help guide teachers in the journey from *information* to *replication*. Each of these stages can be manageable when intentionally taking each area, together with a mentor, and mapping out your own individualized pathway, just like you would do with your own students. Teachers should select a mentor with their own needs in mind. Find someone who has been through the journey and can help avoid the pitfalls and provide encouragement and advice to move forward. Create your own road map so you have clear, comprehensive goals, just like we do with our students. The change process includes many pieces that are built throughout the journey toward CBE. Here's a quick view of a teacher's road map to implement CBE in your classroom (figure 4.14).

These next six figures are consistent through the CBE Ignited implementation process. We want to model what we expect to see happen in the classroom with your students—to preassess (provide information and then readiness) to determine where you are in your journey toward full CBE implementation. This process continues as it becomes routine, where you refine and continually reflect on ways to improve, just as learning continues with our students. The CBE road maps can be complex, just as a whole curriculum can be complex to your students; so we break it down and scaffold it to be manageable. This simpler version includes many pieces that are built throughout the journey toward CBE.

The first step is awareness (see figure 4.15). Understand your current plan of what you will be teaching for the future. Use scope and sequence to ensure effective instruction, professional development, and so on. Understand the difference between a traditional classroom, a flipped classroom, and a competency-based classroom and communicate this with all stakeholders when the time is right.

Once you have seen the possibilities of CBE and are curious about how to make it happen, check to see if you're really ready to embark on this journey as a leader within

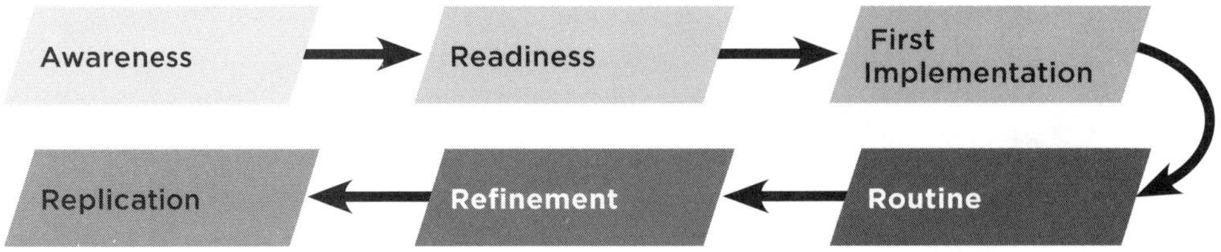

Figure 4.14: CBE road map for teachers—Overview.

Awareness

What are the values and beliefs about learning in my classroom?

- Why does my classroom need to change?
  (Teachers' beliefs and values around learning)
- How do I know my teaching practices are effective?
- Do my students learn at different rates?
- Are all my students engaged in their learning, and are their needs being met? (Delayed or accelerated in learning)

Awareness → Readiness → First Implementation → Routine → Refinement → Replication

Next Steps:

- Follow up with CBE Ignited team and coach.
- Speak with other principals who have done this and hear about their successes and challenges.
- Share ideas with your school & district leadership teams.

Figure 4.15: CBE road map for classrooms—Awareness.

your own classroom. This is the second stage: readiness (see figure 4.16). It's the right thing to do for your students; but unless you have a whole system to support you, it may be tough to implement. Select a mentor to help coach, train, model tools and processes, and avoid the feeling of isolation as you begin the journey. The good news is that you will see immediate results with your students' engagement and will marvel at the learning that happens. Your mentor can help prepare you for the predictable setbacks and ensure your success and the success of your students.

Once you are sure you are ready, you will learn how to use the tools and processes to begin one step at a time with a mentor and start integrating these into your classroom. This stage is called first implementation (figure 4.17, page 106). Each step should be guided carefully so you have a clear road map of where you are going, how you want to get to the next step, and how to assess your success or need for tweaking what is going on. Consider how you present lessons to your students and then allow them to practice. In each step, you are assessing how they are doing and what adjustments they need to make in order to take the next step. The same is true for implementing a new way of education where time is the variable and mastery is the constant.

Now you have started the CBE process and know what tools and processes to use for specific situations. Your classroom is like a well-oiled machine, where students self-direct their learning and behaviors and check and adjust as needed. We call this stage routine (figure 4.18, page 107). This is the fun part, where you are not spending your time on discipline and surface-level learning but rather have the time and opportunity to engage students in deeper understanding of concepts as they have hands-on projects that they are passionate about. Their peers help them assess what they learned and question parts that they may have missed or forgotten. Your job, as a facilitator, is to help guide some of the discussions and learning toward deeper investigation.

Just when you think you have it down in your classroom, CBE requires you to reflect on your processes and tools and the effectiveness of your classroom. Using data, you get the chance now to find better ways to do things that will help your students even more. This is the fifth stage, refine (figure 4.19, page 108). There are many CBE tools ready for this step, to dig into your data to see spots that are easy to miss when you're in the trenches, daily, just trying to get through the day. There are plenty of others also on this journey who can help you in addition to your chosen mentor.

As you see success, consider helping others on their journey. This replication stage (figure 4.20, page 109) will help you with your own processes and self-reflection as you teach others.

As teachers, we are role models for our students. Whether we like it or not, and whether we are intentional or not, it happens.

Readiness

Is my classroom ready for change and open to new ideas of what education looks like, feels like, and acts like?

- What are my current strategies to support good teaching and effective learning?
- What are the differences between traditional teaching and CBE?
- Where are my gaps in implementing CBE?
- Where should I begin?

Next Steps:

- Have the SLT participate in CBE training.
- Self-assess your readiness.
- Create a road map and prioritize steps to support CBE in your school.

Figure 4.16: CBE road map for classrooms—Readiness.

First Implementation

Do I have a dedicated SLT to coordinate outside support services and lead the communication, feedback, and reporting of results to all stakeholders?

- What tools and strategies can I implement on Monday?
- What will be my strengths and challenges in implementing my CBE road map?
- When will I be ready for a classroom walkthrough?

Next Steps:

- SLT has 80 percent of all staff committed to adopt CBE.
- SLT supports teachers by providing training and support in recruiting faculty and promoting teacher leaders.
- SLT develops scope and sequence of learning targets with scales, assessments, instructional strategies, and reporting documents supporting best practices.

Figure 4.17: CBE road map for classrooms—First implementation.

Routine

Do we have 80 percent or more of the students supporting the system change to CBE?

- What evidence do I have that shows learner growth?
- What CBE tools and strategies do I implement consistently?
- What adjustments should I make from the classroom walkthrough?

Awareness → **Readiness** → **First Implementation** → **Routine** → Refinement → Replication

Next Steps:

- SLT determines what are the critical changes needed at the school and classroom level.
- SLT adopts a CBE digital platform and uploads all student data, curriculum, assessments, and so on.

Figure 4.18: CBE road map for classrooms—Routine.

Refinement

What are our processes for refining the scope and sequence of learning targets with scales, assessments, instructional strategies, and reporting documents based on results?

- Are my learners accelerating in their learning?
- What tools and processes have I revised based on learner results?
- How do I make adjustments when learners are not engaged, are struggling, or need acceleration?

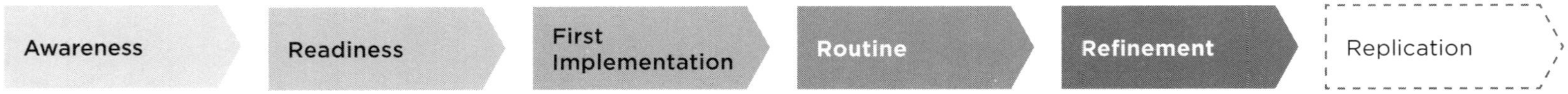

Next Steps:

- Organize documents to be able to share your story.

Figure 4.19: CBE road map for classrooms—Refinement.

Replication

Are we ready to share our stories locally, regionally, and internationally?

- What is my personal compelling story to share?
- What do I need to continue my growth as a trainer, coach, and mentor?
- How do I sustain our innovation and continued improvement?
- How should I share my classroom with others?

Awareness → **Readiness** → **First Implementation** → **Routine** → **Refinement** → **Replication**

Next Steps:

- Utilize the LMS to review the shared vision, targets, and pacing.
- Create multiple ways to communicate progress and challenging areas including strategies for moving forward.
- Learn strategies for integrating social-emotional learning and the heart for each student.

Figure 4.20: CBE road map for classrooms—Replication.

What Are the Takeaways From This Chapter?

Above all, don't be afraid to be real with your students. They appreciate it when they see their hero (you) fail but not give up. Your students can learn the growth mindset of not giving up but being encouraged when lessons are challenging because it means they are learning. Their greatest need is to be heard, understood, and appreciated. You can show this to them daily in your actions.

Over the years, we have had the privilege of working with amazing teachers throughout the United States and in other countries. Young and old, the common factor has been a passion and love for their students and a desire to improve their lives. They believe that all students can learn and change based on research-based best practices. It's inspiring to see our students engage and get excited when they learn something new. Often, we can step back and allow them to work through the stages as we guide them to resources, ideas, and what research may have already been done. Having real projects that affect real people is key for feeling like you are part of something greater. A big mistake we have seen is not providing enough structure to ensure success. It's a fine line to walk—to support but not control everything. We want to help you on a journey that we celebrate, as you see success along the way. It's hard work but well worth it. Everything you do will also model the same process we expect from your students, from leaders, and from other stakeholders. We will follow a road map that is not always linear. You will help guide your journey by your own personal interests, opportunities, and curiosity. We invite you to join the CBE community and transform your classroom environment and learning experiences for your students.

CBE Lesson Plan Template

Title:

Grade Level:	Content Area:

Overview:

Brief description:

Learning Targets (Standards)

Cross-Curricular Connection (Show how the lesson is used to address other content areas.)

Assessments (Insert or attach rubric for project-based, analytical learning. If skill-based, provide assessment or preassessment. This should show what mastery looks like in the Proficient column and beyond mastery in the Advanced column.)

Target	Advanced	Proficient	Developing	Emerging

Materials (Differentiate between required and desired *and* type of resource: book, website, handout, and so on.) **Books:** **Website:** **Handouts or Attachments:**
Daily Delivery (For example, prior knowledge activation, guided or independent practice, activities, group work, and so on.) Day One (For example, preassessment activity or the hook that gets students interested and activates prior learning.) **Direct Instruction:** **Modeling:** **Checking for Understanding:** **Closure:** **Independent Practice:**
Attachments (Attach or paste assessments, handouts, visuals, and so on.)

CHAPTER 5

Principal Perspective

It may seem easier to do things alone, but there's strength in a team moving forward together. Principals have the responsibility of leading that team at the schoolwide level. Leaders who have carefully read the first four chapters of this book, including the student and teacher perspective chapters (pages 41 and 73, respectively), should by now have a good idea of what goes on in a CBE classroom. They know what they are asking their schools to undertake. Implementing CBE at the schoolwide level is challenging but rewarding, and it takes a leader who is willing to be courageous and develop certain characteristics.

The essential questions this chapter answers include the following.

- What are important factors for principals in a CBE system?
- What does the principal perspective look like in CBE?
- What does the school road map to CBE implementation look like?
- What are the takeaways from this chapter?

What Are Important Factors for Principals in a CBE System?

The core foundation of successful principals is the deep desire to do what is right for all students and support their teachers along the way. This starts with asking the tough questions, especially when they don't have the answers.

1. What can we learn from analyzing quantitative data about student achievement, learning gaps, and the commitment and focus on equity in our school?
2. What do we know about the school climate and culture from qualitative and empirical data from observations and experiences?

3. What do our former students tell us about their learning successes and challenges?
4. What is the evidence that we are meeting the academic, personal, and social needs of every student?
5. What levels of intervention are in place when students are not successful?
6. What happens when students are ready to move at a faster pace?
7. What are the characteristics of a teaching and learning system that could meet the needs of all students?

Effective principals facilitate a highly collaborative school leadership team (SLT) composed of teacher leaders and subject-area specialists. After exploring these questions and reflecting on the answers, the SLT members have the information to assist the principal in taking this initial conversation to the entire faculty and staff. Once these tough questions are asked, it will become apparent that the next reflection required is the exploration of the values and beliefs of the faculty and staff with regard to learning. Identifying and embracing essential core values and beliefs about learning is essential to beginning the CBE journey. CBE schools share a set of beliefs that both unite staff and students and guide the work. Successful CBE schools engage all stakeholders in discussions of core beliefs and values around teaching and learning, as these are the foundation for transforming a traditional school to a CBE system.

Common beliefs and values that support CBE include the following.

- All students are unique, need to understand themselves, and must build positive relations with peers and adults.
- Learning is about developing the mental, emotional, and physical dimensions of each student.
- Every student learns at a different rate.
- All students need to be deeply engaged in their learning.
- We need to prepare students for their future.
- Learning needs to be transparent in that it can happen anywhere, anyplace, and anytime.
- When all these conditions are in place, students will accelerate in both the amount and the depth of their learning.

- Students should have voice and choice in their learning, and when ready, students should control their learning plans and create ambitious goals to achieve successful outcomes.

In traditional schools, many of these values and beliefs are not part of the culture. Despite the vision of No Child Left Behind (www2.ed.gov/nclb/landing.jhtml), the Every Student Succeeds Act (ESSA; www.ed.gov/essa?src=rn), and significant investment of resources, coupled with the commitment of inspired educators to bring equity and opportunity for all students, there continue to be unacceptable achievement gaps and disproportionate dropout rates between minority and majority ethnic and racial groups (DoSomething.org, n.d.; NCES, 2023). Part of the explanation behind these data is that schools originally were never intended to educate all students. They were designed using a sort-and-select system created centuries ago to track students into skilled and unskilled employment or the university (Lezotte, 1997). Even with policy recommendations by the OECD (2012), it is a struggle to be sure every student has access and opportunity to learn.

CBE reimagines this antiquated system. It's real, sweeping change, and principals need to be ready for a true paradigm shift. This starts with developing a skill set to help ensure success and continues with fully considering the implications of change.

Leadership Skill Set

Today, school principals are asked to meet the needs of all students within an outdated and inefficient classroom learning structure and system. Education is the social-mobility pathway for students, and their success is vital to the country's economic future. The challenge for our schools and leaders is that workforce demands continue to change dramatically. Principals must lead schools that are agile and future-focused to prepare students for their future success, which requires substantive and transformational changes that depart from traditional schooling systems. Systems change is challenging because the inertia of the traditional schooling system is a powerful force. As effective change agents with a vision for implementing CBE, principals need a skill set that supports second-order change (see chapter 6, page 139, for more on second-order change). In chapter 4 (figure 4.1, page 76), we introduced traits that successful CBE teachers should cultivate; leaders need the same skill set with an even wider perspective. Figure 5.1 (page 116) provides a summary.

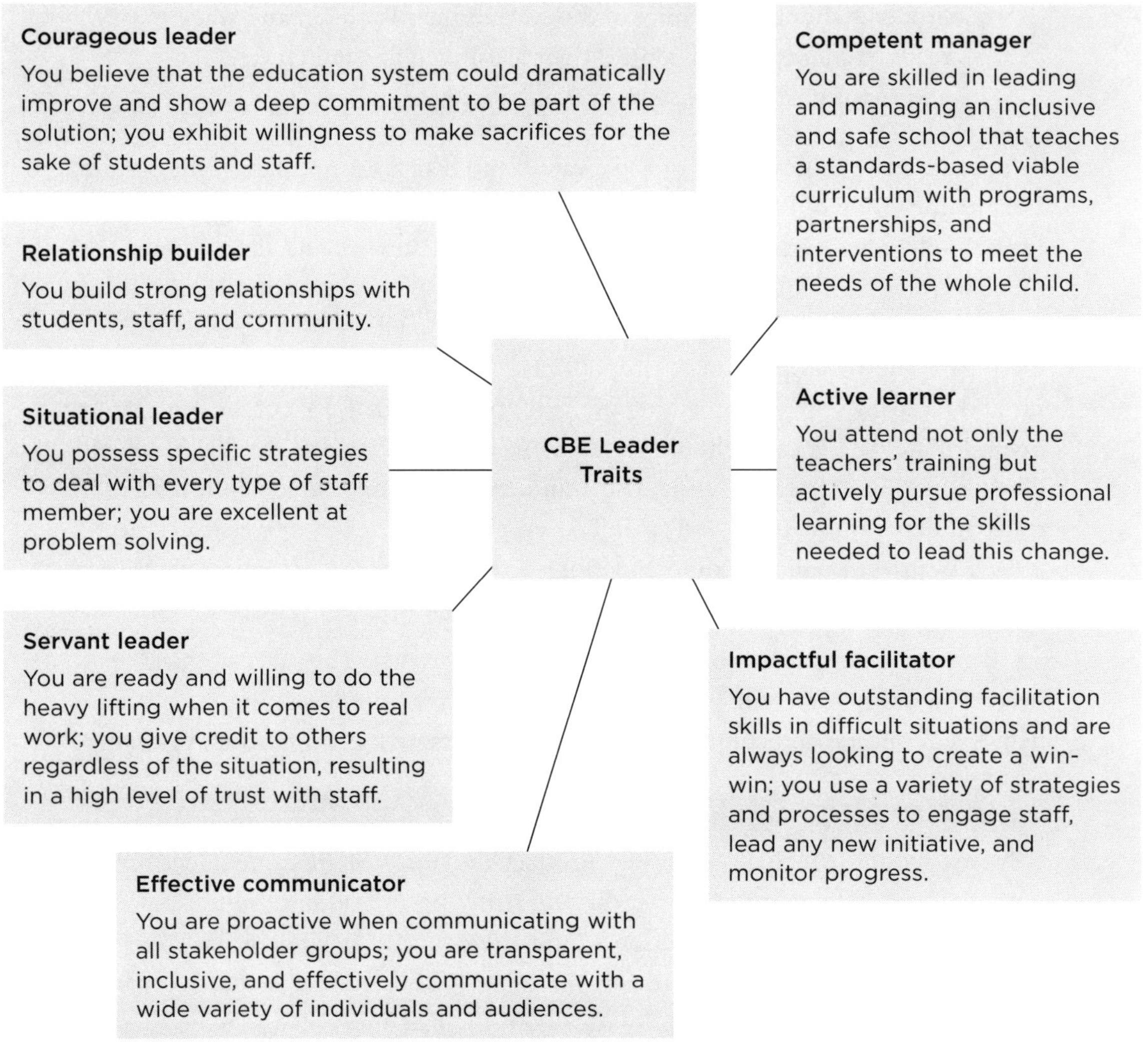

Figure 5.1: Key skill set of successful CBE principals.

Considerations for Change

Change is difficult! The deeper the change, the more difficult it becomes. Changing schools from a traditional time-based to competency-based philosophy requires overhauling many of the structures found in current schools. It is critical to understand the elements of change, especially moving from first-order to second-order change (see chapter 6, page 139). Whether you are the superintendent or a principal, the elements are the same with regard to first-order and second-order change; the main difference is your locus of control. This means decisions such as the district's policies, finance, and curriculum are decided at the district level.

However, decisions like staffing, scheduling, and professional development training are decided at the school level.

Successful principals take the time to not only understand the components of CBE but preplan a strategy to help bring on all their stakeholders. Districts and schools on this journey will share strong sets of beliefs around learning, shared visions, and codes of collaboration. However, where a school differs from a district is that you are the front line of implementation of CBE. Your classrooms and school will look and act differently, and it's up to you to help guide, support, and foster this change. Depending on how progressive your school is, the changes can range from minor alterations (because you already have many of the conditions in place, such as standard-referenced grading) to overhauling almost every aspect of the school. When you have committed to embracing this new paradigm, it is critical you frontload the changes that will be taking place. That means you must first understand what this might look like and then develop a strategy to lead the change in your school.

Here are ten concepts to consider before transitioning into CBE.

1. Clear learning targets with scales in all academic and 21st century skills
2. Clear assessments and instructional guidelines for the learning targets
3. Appropriate scheduling to meet the needs of every student
4. Promotion and acceleration of students
5. Competency-based report cards and honor roll
6. Professional development systems and CBE teacher evaluations
7. Graduation requirements and early entry into universities
8. Grouping and regrouping of students when meeting proficiency levels
9. Eligibility requirements for extracurricular activities
10. Implementing a digital learning management system that supports CBE

Also, there are many other organizations that have years of experience supporting schools making this transition. See appendix A (page 183) for a list.

Successful principals need to have a game plan before diving into this transition. Refer back to the key steps necessary for principals to deploy CBE (figure 2.10, page 31). These elements are time sequenced and will get you started.

The most challenging part is to support all types of staff members while maintaining a healthy climate of trust and support. Whenever change is initiated in any part of the system, in our experience, there are reactions from three different groups of people. Principals need to have strategies to address all three groups.

1. **Omnivores (20 percent):** They have been waiting for this change and will do anything and everything to make it successful.
2. **Missouri-ites (60 percent):** They are the show-me people. They need to have locally driven, tangible proof that this is better than what they are presently doing. Hard evidence is often helpful to change minds, but it is hard to come by. The flip side is that once these practitioners commit, they are thoughtful, diligent in the implementation of the change, and confident in the path ahead.
3. **Naysayers (20 percent):** They resist anything new for a plethora of reasons, but they are critical stakeholders, because the ones who finally do recognize success and commit become the gatekeepers and fiercely protect the changes for the future.

Richard developed this grouping; other change experts have come up with similar notions to categorize groups within a school, such as Anthony Muhammad's (2017) believers, fundamentalists, tweeners, and survivors from his book *Transforming School Culture*.

What Does the Principal Perspective Look Like in CBE?

The role of a school principal will change significantly because the classrooms will change, and the highest priority for a school leader is providing direction and support for teachers to be successful. Principals need to be dedicated and agile learners who seek to understand every aspect of CBE.

Figure 5.2 displays the typical progressions a teacher will experience and visual outcomes that principals will be looking to see. Each quadrant represents a progression aligned with the road map stages that principals can watch for as they carry out their walkthroughs.

When a principal begins to do classroom walkthroughs, there are several levels of implementation that should be visible in each classroom. It is important that this will be a journey for every teacher. Each school needs a clear teacher matrix of implementation. Our goal with CBE is helping every student have more voice and choice in their learning, and this sample matrix is a simple illustration of some key elements.

Transforming a school from a traditional model to a CBE system requires in-depth, ongoing professional development and coaching. During initial training, principals and central office personnel are asked to take on new roles, which can be both scary and unpredictable. Most administrators have never taught in a competency-based classroom, and now they are charged with leading their schools

Readiness

Good traditional teaching (five-step lesson plan)

Shared vision

Code of collaboration

Standard operating procedures; tools and processes

Unpacking the learning and making this visible on the walls (scales written in students' terminology, rubrics, and so on)

First Implementation

Voice and choice in simple ways

Classroom differentiation from direct instruction with learning stations and other choices

Data-driven decision making

Goal setting

Introduce the digital platform

Routine

Monitor the vision and code

Digital platform in practice with playlist

Gradual release of control from teacher directed to student directed

Acceleration of learning

Cool projects

Refinement

Refine all the processes

Students take more ownership of their learning

Students create their own playlist

Students create their own schedule

Results are accelerated (three years' growth in one year's time)

Figure 5.2: Progress of CBE classrooms.

on this challenging journey. Many of them were experienced in administrative leadership positions, and for the most part, they were simply trying to survive in the traditional system with all the demands placed on them. Now they are being asked to take on this transformation and be the point person in ensuring its success.

As with any new initiative that comes along, it's easy to believe in the possibility that there is a better way of doing things. The challenge comes when moving from philosophy to action. The difficult part is learning this for the first time, and the principal must lead a school in this shift away from everything faculty, staff, and students are familiar and comfortable with. Many school principals embrace change and are remarkably adaptable to this new paradigm, while other school leaders struggle greatly with the transition. Our focus with the CBE Ignited approach is to help principals see how their leadership role will evolve, and understand the tools and processes necessary to transform a school system.

First, we help them understand what it means to be an effective leader in this new system. We look at the attributes of leadership in a traditional time-based system and then in a competency-based system. At this point, you can be a competent leader in a traditional system and struggle when trying to transition into this new system. It takes a different skill set that we help guide. The main reason this change is difficult is that we are asking all stakeholders, but especially teachers, to be immersed in an entirely different role—a role they have never experienced either as a learner or as a teacher. At times, this change process can be overwhelming.

The same can be said for the administrators because we are asking them to lead this transition in which they have little or no experience. Administrators will need to change everything from attendance policies to teacher evaluations. The major responsibility for a principal is evaluating the staff. The teacher evaluation process in a competency classroom is very different from a traditional one. In fact, there are highly skilled teachers in a traditional system who may not meet the standards and proficiencies in the CBE teacher and student process. In a traditional classroom, we are looking for compliant and attentive students, and this is not always the case in a CBE classroom. The focus is on the learning and engagement of the students. In fact, during much of the CBE teacher observation, the principal spends time interviewing students, which rarely happens in a traditional classroom observation.

The following narrative, a composite of many principals' real journeys, helps illustrate how these changes might look.

> *John is a dedicated teacher and administrator, and his passion for students and their well-being carries over into the community, where he is actively involved in the Rotary Club and other volunteer service. He regularly attends local sports games, supporting his children in elementary, middle, and high school basketball, baseball, and football. He loves his new position as a middle school principal and embraces the sometimes stressful duty of keeping everyone safe while ensuring quality learning is happening. The new district initiative for a competency-based system provides opportunities for community leaders to get involved in his school, as they are tackling real-world problems that his students can assist with as solutionaries while mastering some of their required skills.*
>
> *The faculty at John's middle school are a mix of traditional educators and some young, energetic educators who had very wild ideas at times. This year, the teachers and staff worked together for two days to create a new vision and mission for the school and determine goals and timelines for implementing CBE that could realistically and optimally be achieved. The wordsmithing was grueling, but in the end, everyone felt a sense of ownership and accomplishment and pride, feeling like they now had a common vision and clear goals that everyone had a stake in.*

It was challenging for John to help everyone keep to the shared vision, but doing the work up front really made a difference for them in the first year of implementation. He had never worked in an environment where there were thirty days of professional development each year. He watched teachers get excited about collaborating on themes and projects, and the school environment turned into a very positive place to be each day.

John glances in the teachers' lounge as he walks by on his way to his office. He notices several teachers looking over the code of collaboration they had put on a poster to remind them about team dynamics and the importance of communication and collaboration. Their willingness to try new things gives John a sense of pride in the faculty and staff that he has been privileged to work with this year. He knew they were trusting his leadership to support them, and that students were also aware of the change process and the impact on their roles as learners.

It is time to start his morning rounds, like every good principal he has ever seen. Instead of just positive feedback, he is learning to measure growth and accountability for each of the teachers in the areas they have identified as their individual weekly priority. John is pleased to see students able to navigate their own learning with choices clearly designated. His teachers often have visitors from other schools who observe their graphic organizers as well as assessment tools that are displayed for transparency of the learning expectations. John remembers his own classroom observations when the principal would sometimes give him glowing remarks or harsh criticism but rarely offer solutions. John is determined to support his teachers with relevant and continuous feedback and to develop into a highly effective instructional leader.

Back in his office, John pulls up his dashboard in the LMS so he can see the overall health of his school, with a control meter on safety, learning, and discipline. It is great to see the students so involved in helping ensure everyone supports the culture of respect for all that was established at the start of the school year. The student and staff weekly check-in for CORE Court is like a well-oiled machine that needs adjustments at times but keeps the school moving forward in a positive direction.

John also has a dashboard for his own learning and collaboration. It is nice to be able to talk weekly with other administrators who struggle with some of the same issues, and also have some consultants who help facilitate research-based solutions for the groups. John feels more supported and is growing professionally better than in any other place he has worked.

What Does the School Road Map to CBE Implementation Look Like?

The purpose of the school road map is to provide a scope and sequence of events that are necessary to implement CBE at the school level. There are many elements that are occurring simultaneously. It is important to remember that even though principals are the primary person responsible for implementation, it is critical that they share the responsibilities with their staff.

The CBE school road map (figure 5.3) provides insight into the different progression levels to undertake. In the following series of figures, we highlight each stage of the road map. Then we provide a sample of a road map document that a school might use and follow as it progresses.

In the first stage, awareness, you understand your district's current strategic plan and vision for the future. Understand your school's historical and current situation in terms of student achievement, collegiality among staff, school climate, standard operating procedures, effective instruction, professional development, and so on. Understand the difference between a traditional school and a competency-based school and communicate this with all stakeholders when the time is right. See figure 5.4 (page 124).

Administer the CBE readiness survey or similar screening tool in the second stage, readiness, to examine the overall school climate and determine your school's current levels of readiness for change. The goal is to get a 360-degree view of the school. The CBEIgnited.org website offers the full survey; the following list is a sampling of the survey questions.

- What is the overall performance of your students as it relates to achievement data?
- What is the overall performance of your staff as it relates to professional development growth?
- What is the relation between the administration, staff, community, parents, and others?
- At what level of collaboration would you score your school?
- What are some initiatives that you have initiated and completed?
- What were the results of those?
- What is your understanding of CBE as it relates to changes that will happen in your school?
- What will be the biggest challenges in adopting a CBE mindset?

See figure 5.5 (page 125) for an overview of the readiness stage.

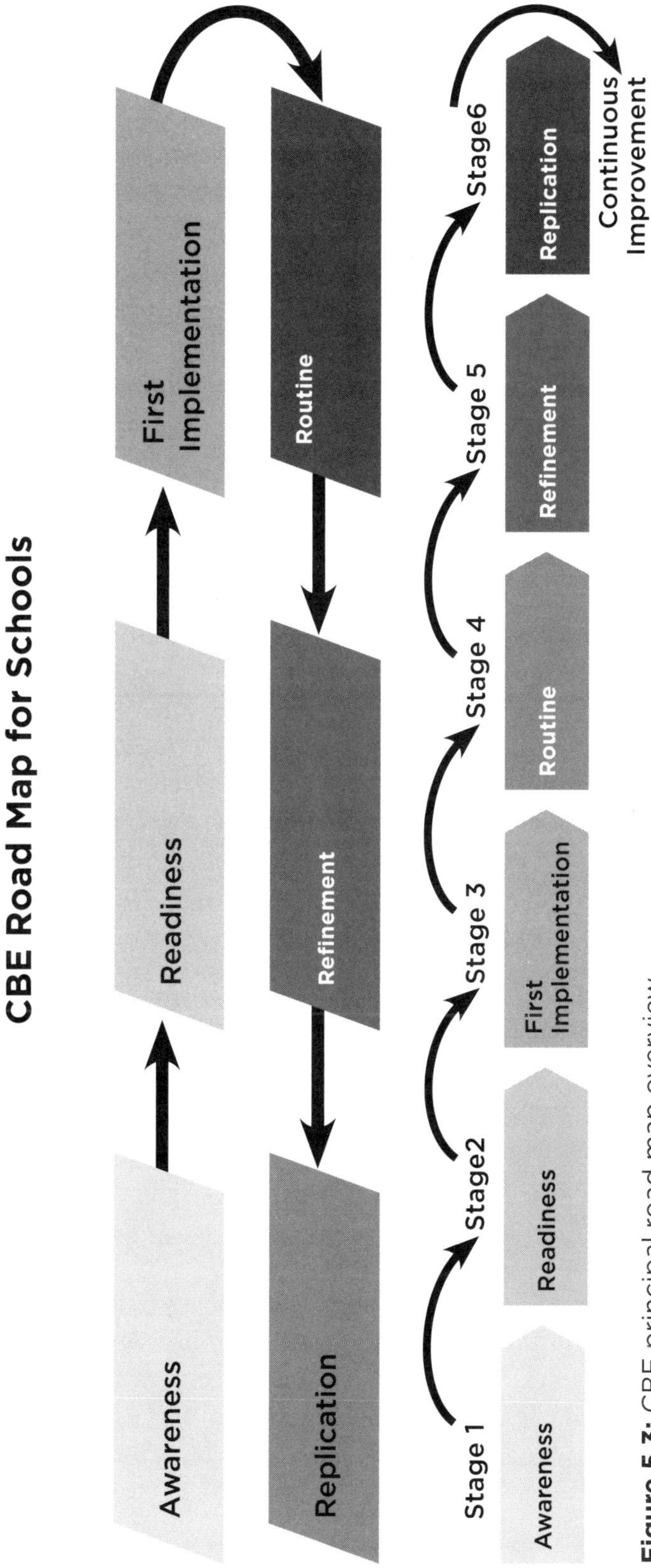

Figure 5.3: CBE principal road map overview.

Awareness

What are the values and beliefs about learning in our school?

- What are our values and beliefs around learning?
- What does our student achievement, climate, culture, and so on, over time look like?
- How does our current school align to our values and beliefs? For example, do our students learn at different rates, are all our students' needs being met (delayed or accelerated in learning), and are all students actively engaged in learning?
- How does a CBE system align to our values and beliefs?
- What are some immediate things we can change?
- What are some long-term things we can do?

Awareness → **Readiness** → **First Implementation** → Routine → Refinement → Replication

Next Steps:

- Utilize the LMS to review the shared vision, targets, and pacing.
- Create multiple ways to communicate progress and challenging areas including strategies for moving forward.
- Learn strategies for integrating social-emotional learning and the heart for each student. Follow up with CBE Ignited team and coach.
- Speak with other principals who have done this and hear about their successes and challenges.
- Share ideas with your SLT and DLT.

Figure 5.4: Principal road map—Awareness.

Readiness

Is my school ready for change and open to new ideas of what education looks like, feels like, and acts like?

- What are our values and beliefs around learning?
- What does our student achievement, climate, culture, and so on, over time look like?
- How does our current school align to our values and beliefs? For example, do our students learn at different rates, are all our students' needs being met (delayed or accelerated in learning), and are all students actively engaged in learning?
- How does a CBE system align to our values and beliefs?
- What are some immediate things we can change?
- What are some long-term things we can do? How satisfied is our staff with the culture of our school?
- What are the components of CBE, and how will roles change?
- How will implementing a quality CBE system meet our students' needs?
- What are the characteristics of a quality CBE teacher?
- Do we have a principal and teachers ready to move forward?
- What should a day in the life of a CBE learner look like?
- Do we have a guaranteed and viable curriculum?
- Do we have the capacity to transition to a CBE system?
- What are our strengths and barriers of moving toward CBE?
- What can we learn from other schools implementing CBE?
- What will our CBE road map look like?

Next Steps:

- Have your SLT participate in CBE training.
- Self-assess your readiness.
- Create a road map and prioritize steps to support CBE in your school.

Figure 5.5: Principal road map—Readiness.

In the third stage, the first implementation, develop or refine the SLT to help create a shared vision and code of collaboration with all staff and stakeholders, including students, based on the district's shared vision. Create, prioritize, and implement the school road map moving toward CBE.

Successful principals follow their road map and check and adjust as needed. Principals will be looking for different deliverables than in a traditional classroom (for example, shared vision statements, codes of collaboration, learning outcome progress charts, and standard operating procedures). Principals are responsible to create and deploy classroom walkthroughs that capture what a CBE classroom should look like; these are critical for principals to ensure CBE fidelity. In the beginning, a handful of teachers are trained in CBE; they will need external feedback to keep them on course. It is critical that principals attend training so they feel confident in providing feedback in this type of classroom. See figure 5.6.

In the fourth stage, routine, 80 percent of staff are committed; this involves determining the roles and responsibilities of staff and stakeholder groups to support the school road map and, when they are ready, empowering them to help make decisions. Oversee the deployment of the road map with regular updates and check and adjust as needed. The school's shared vision and code of collaboration are critical to a successful implementation because they provide the leverage to support staff and also to hold them accountable. The process to arrive at the school's code of collaboration is the same as what students and teachers use to create classroom codes of collaboration; see figure 3.9 (page 59) for an example. Effective leaders begin with a tight-tight approach, meaning they make the critical decisions at the start. But once the school reaches the routine level, it is important to gradually release control of leadership, depending on the readiness level of the teachers. Faculty and staff need to be empowered to assess and give input on the readiness level and timelines for implementation. For example, effective staff meetings initially should be designed and created by the principal, but as teachers become more skilled and confident with CBE, they will want to take on more leadership roles, and effective principals plan for this. Quality education systems provide the opportunity for individual growth for every staff member. This is important to not only sustain the journey but also allow for a new generation of leaders. See figure 5.7 (page 128).

First Implementation

Do we have a dedicated leadership team to coordinate outside support services and lead the communication, feedback, reporting, and results to all stakeholders?

- What does our readiness survey tell us?
- What is the process for our shared vision and code of collaboration and road map?
- What should we be measuring to show improvement?
- What is the process to communicate this change to all stakeholders?
- What will our initial school's CBE road map look like?
- What are the internal and external barriers of moving toward CBE?
- How will CBE impact our instructional delivery, curriculum, digital platform, and assessment practices?

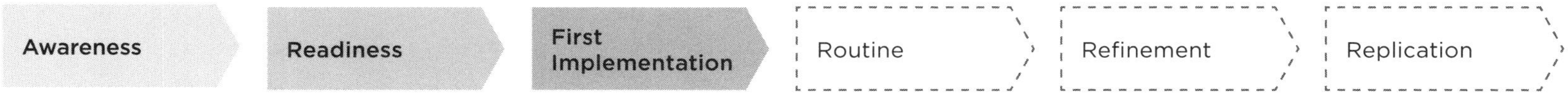

Next Steps:

- SLT has 80 percent of all staff committed to adopt CBE.
- SLT supports teachers by providing training and support in recruiting faculty and promoting teacher leaders.
- SLT develops scope and sequence of learning targets with scales, assessments, instructional strategies, and reporting documents supporting best practices.

Figure 5.6: Principal road map—First implementation.

Routine

Do we have 80 percent or more of the total stakeholders supporting the system change to CBE?

- What tools and processes do we need to deploy throughout the school to support CBE?
- What adjustments do we need on our CBE road map?
- What is the process to conduct school and classroom walkthroughs?
- How will we communicate our vision and growth to all stakeholders?

Next Steps:

- SLT determines what are the critical changes needed at the school and classroom levels.
- SLT adopts a CBE digital platform and uploads all student data, curriculum, assessments, and so on.

Figure 5.7: Principal road map—Routine.

You have 100 percent of staff committed and are actively practicing CBE in your school and classrooms. You are now in the fifth stage, refining your processes based on data, and have made several progressions. You have established a CBE culture and continue to improve in all areas. Regularly celebrate successes and commit to continuous improvement of the school by asking the difficult questions and empowering your staff. Once your school reaches the refinement level, it is necessary to consider how the school will recruit, train, evaluate, and promote new faculty and staff members. Once they begin reaching higher levels on the teacher road map, they will be looking for new leadership opportunities. We encourage schools to define the pathways for teacher leadership, and then provide those experiences.

Finally, when certain benchmarks on the school road map are attained and the deliverables have been reached, it is important to celebrate often and with sincerity because the staff will begin to understand the power of CBE and that it is transforming the learning environment and supporting student success. See figure 5.8 (page 130).

The sixth stage, replication, is about telling your story and being willing to help others on their journey. See figure 5.9 (page 131).

This is a progression of events over time that successful CBE schools have adopted. Yours might look different depending on your situation and readiness level; however, it is critical that there is some sort of continuum of implementation that will guide your transition. Figure 5.10 (page 132) provides a sample school road map document.

It is also important to realize that, besides the school's road map, teachers (see chapter 4, page 73) and districts (see chapter 6, page 139) will need to have their own road map to expedite this transition.

Refinement

What are our processes for refining the scope and sequence of learning targets with scales, assessments, instructional strategies, and reporting documents based on results?

- What is our process to continually get better in reaching our vision?
- How and when should we re-energize our shared vision?
- How do we collect data and processes to tell our story?
- Does our human resources system support CBE and include recruiting, training, evaluating, and promoting educators?
- What will we do to keep our best talent?
- What documents, artifacts, videos, and anecdotes should we be collecting?

Next Steps:

- Organize documents to be able to share your story.

Figure 5.8: Principal road map—Refinement.

Replication

Are we ready to share our stories locally, regionally, and internationally?

- Do we have a compelling story to share?
- How do we sustain our innovation and continued improvement?
- How should we share our classrooms and schools with others?

Next Steps:

- Utilize the LMS to review the shared vision, targets, and pacing.
- Create multiple ways to communicate progress and challenging areas including strategies moving forward.
- Learn strategies for integrating social-emotional learning and the heart for each student.

Figure 5.9: Principal road map—Replication.

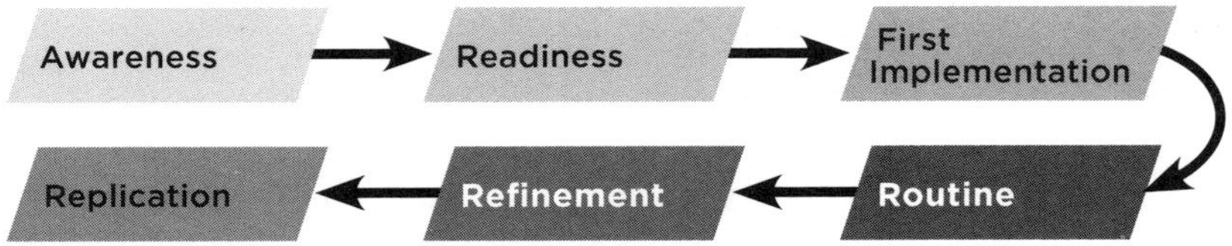

Critical Questions	Tools and Strategies	Critical Components	Changes Needed	Timeline and Deliverables
Awareness Level *(These are the critical questions that need to be answered.)*				
• What are your values and beliefs around learning? • What does our student achievement, climate, culture, and so on, over time look like? • How does our current school align to our values and beliefs? For example, do our students learn at different rates, are all our students' needs being met (delayed or accelerated in learning), and are all students actively engaged in learning? • How does a CBE system align to our values and beliefs? • What are some immediate things we can change? • What are some long-term things we can do?	• What are some tools and strategies needed to transition to CBE *(parking lot, standard operating procedures, plus-delta, affinity diagram, power voting, root cause analysis, think-pair-share, Pareto chart, goal setting, commit-o-gram, T-chart)*?	• What are the critical components of CBE, and what does this look like in the school and classroom *(time-based versus competency-based advancement, growth mindset, effective traditional teaching, shared vision, code of collaboration, learning targets with scales, project-based learning, instructional delivery, assessments and reporting of progress, digital platform)*?	• What changes will the school need to make to adopt CBE *(guaranteed and viable curriculum, scheduling, promotion of students, report card, honor roll, graduation requirements, situational grouping, grading, acceleration of students, eligibility requirements, and so on)*?	• What is a realistic timeline to implement this with fidelity in our school? ▪ 10 percent of the staff ▪ 80 percent of the staff ▪ 100 percent of the staff • What are the key deliverables for CBE implementation? ▪ Staff can identify the critical components of CBE. ▪ Staff have agreed upon values and beliefs around learning.

Critical Questions	Tools and Strategies	Critical Components	Changes Needed	Timeline and Deliverables
Readiness Level *(These are the initial elements that need to be in place before moving forward: Principal needs to be committed for a school to move forward.)*				
• How satisfied is our staff with the culture of our school? • What are the components of CBE, and how will roles change? • How will implementing a quality CBE system meet our students' needs? • What are the characteristics of a quality CBE teacher? • Do we have a principal and teachers ready to move forward? • What should a day in the life of a CBE learner look like? • Do we have a guaranteed and viable curriculum? • Do we have the capacity to transition to a CBE system? • What are our strengths and barriers of moving toward CBE? • What can we learn from other schools implementing CBE? • What will our CBE road map look like?	• Principal needs to understand first- and second-order change. • Principal needs to understand how to use tools effectively to move toward more effective schools *(parking lot, standard operating procedures, plus-delta, affinity diagram, power voting, root cause analysis, think-pair-share, Pareto chart, goal setting, commit-o-gram, T-chart)*.	• Principal needs to understand the difference between traditional schools and CBE schools. • Leadership team needs to implement a CBE readiness report to determine their next steps to implement CBE. • Leadership team needs to complete a gap analysis between current practices and CBE. • Principal needs to create a leadership team. • Principal needs to understand the current status of the district and school's vision.	• Analyze the results of the feedback report to determine opportunities and challenges to implement CBE. • Communicate results to staff and steps to move toward vision. • Examine components to determine what changes will be needed to move toward CBE *(guaranteed and viable curriculum, scheduling, promotion of students, report card, honor roll, graduation requirements, situational grouping, grading, acceleration of students, eligibility requirements, and so on)*.	• One to three months: ▪ Principal needs to communicate effectively with all stakeholders to help them understand CBE ***(staff, parents, students, and community)***. ▪ Leadership team needs 10 percent of staff committed to training and 80 percent to be willing to learn more. • Deliverables: ▪ Readiness survey results ▪ Communication plan ▪ Establishment of a leadership team

Figure 5.10: Sample school road map.

continued →

Critical Questions	Tools and Strategies	Critical Components	Changes Needed	Timeline and Deliverables
First Implementation Level The Rubicon Effect *(This is where some classroom shifts to a CBE leadership team are led by the principal.)*				
• What does our readiness survey tell us? • What is the process for our shared vision and code of collaboration and road map? • What should we be measuring to show improvement? • What is the process to communicate this change to all stakeholders? • What will our initial school's CBE road map look like? • What are the internal and external barriers of moving toward CBE? • How will CBE impact our instructional delivery, curriculum, digital platform, and assessments practices?	• School administrators needs to attend and participate in all CBE trainings. • Leadership team needs to be using effective tools *(parking lot, standard operating procedures, flow charts, plan-do-check-adjust, plus-delta, power voting, root cause analysis, staff collaboration scale, think-pair-share, Pareto chart, goal setting, commit-o-gram)*. • Leadership team creates a process to communicate effectively with all stakeholders to help them understand CBE *(staff, parents, students, and community)*.	• Leadership team needs to create, deploy, and share the road map and timelines for CBE deployment. • Leadership team needs to understand and deploy a plan-do-check-adjust cycle to support CBE. • Vision statement and code of collaboration are visible with a process to measure. • List of standard operating procedures is visible. • Evidence of learning is visible throughout the school.	• School administrators need to support the early adopters by deploying classroom walkthroughs. • When ready, school administrators need to administer a commitment-o-gram to determine staff commitment *(80 percent of the staff needs to be committed)*. • Schools need a shared vision and code of collaboration visible. • Leadership team needs to create, deploy, and support training to support CBE.	• Three to six months: ▪ Leadership team needs to communicate with all stakeholder groups on the progress. ▪ Leadership team needs greater than 80 percent of staff and at least three model classrooms. • Deliverables: ▪ CBE road map ▪ Shared vision and code of collaboration ▪ Principal participates in CBE training ▪ 10 percent of staff trained and implementing CBE

Critical Questions	Tools and Strategies	Critical Components	Changes Needed	Timeline and Deliverables
Routine Level *(This is when 80 percent of classrooms are deploying CBE effectively.)*				
• What tools and processes do we need to deploy throughout the school to support CBE? • What adjustments do we need on our CBE road map? • What is the process to conduct school and classroom walkthroughs? • How will we communicate our vision and growth to all stakeholders?	• Leadership team needs to communicate the road map and timelines for CBE with staff. • Leadership team needs to adopt or create a school tool book to support CBE. • Leadership team needs to adopt quality guidelines (for example, total quality management) to ensure that the vision, code of collaboration, and implementation of CBE is being deployed with fidelity.	• 80 percent of teachers need to understand and deploy a plan-do-check-adjust cycle that supports the road map. • Positive results must be demonstrated in critical areas of the shared vision. • Digital platform needs to be investigated.	• Leadership team needs to build staff capacity to do classroom walkthroughs. • Leadership team needs to revisit and re-energize the shared vision and code of collaboration.	• Six to twelve months: ▪ Leadership team needs 80 percent of staff committed to training. ▪ Leadership team needs to regularly celebrate their journey. ▪ Proof of concept needs to have been attained and validated by outside parties. • Deliverables: ▪ CBE road map updated with data collection ▪ Shared vision and code of collaboration measured ▪ Classroom and school walkthroughs established ▪ 80 percent of staff trained

continued →

Critical Questions	Tools and Strategies	Critical Components	Changes Needed	Timeline and Deliverables
Refinement Level *(This is proof of concept for the entire school; plus two years ongoing; 100 percent of teachers.)*				
• What is our process to continually get better in reaching our vision? • How and when should we re-energize our shared vision? • How do we collect data and processes to tell our story? • Does our human resources system support CBE and include recruiting, training, evaluating, and promoting our educators? • What will we do to keep our best talent? • What documents, artifacts, videos, and anecdotes should we be collecting?	• School administrators identify the best facilitators to help support with training and classroom walkthroughs. • Leadership team is committed to improving the results by analyzing relevant data and making adjustments.	• 100 percent of teachers are trained, and some show positive trend data related to the school and class vision. • Teachers are working collaboratively to improve data for all students. • Digital platform needs to be implemented.	• Leadership team should collect policies, schedules, tools, and processes used. • School administrators should collect and verify positive trend data that support learner achievements and facilitator effectiveness. • School administrators need to review the road map and make adjustments.	• One to three years: ▪ Leadership team needs 100 percent of staff committed to training. ▪ Leadership team needs to refine their induction and training to attract new educators. • Deliverables: ▪ CBE road map updated ▪ Refinement of all tools and processes driven by results ▪ Process created for hiring, training, evaluating, retaining, and promoting staff ▪ Digital platform implemented ▪ 100 percent of staff trained

Critical Questions	Tools and Strategies	Critical Components	Changes Needed	Timeline and Deliverables
Replication Level *(This is proof of concept for scaling; sharing your story and inviting other schools.)*				
• Do we have a compelling story to share? • How do we sustain our innovation and continued improvement? • How should we share our classrooms and school with others?	• Leadership team should be willing to share their story that includes tools, processes, curriculum, grouping, promotion, and so on.	• Principal and teachers document their journey to share with others. • Principals open their schools to visitors. • Teachers open their classrooms to other teachers within their school. • Teachers open their classrooms to teachers outside their school.	• School administrators should be willing to open their school and classrooms for others. • School administrators should be willing to host training sessions.	• Two to five years: ▪ Leadership team needs to build a systematic recruitment cycle to certify, train, evaluate, and promote new educators. • Deliverables: ▪ CBE road map updated ▪ Results-driven story documented ▪ Process to share your journey with others

What Are the Takeaways From This Chapter?

Principals who are ready to commit to the deep and lasting change that CBE promises are in for a journey—there's no shortcut. With the support of the SLT, principals can work with teachers and students to find success on that journey. There's never been a more rewarding one. It begins with conversations and exploration to assess readiness and continues until principals have realized a dynamic school community where students take the lead on their own learning. If stakeholders truly believe in student learning for *all*, this journey is the answer.

Developing and refining the traits that ensure success and embracing change are the most important factors for leaders in a CBE system. When they do, they can successfully do the work of creating and following a comprehensive school road map to a competency-based system. The next chapter explores how this journey looks at the district level.

CHAPTER 6

Superintendent Perspective

You can't provide a new solution when educators don't see there is a problem. This chapter unlocks some of the mystery behind what type of educational leader can be successful in implementing CBE and encourages others to become more aware of CBE. The ultimate goal of the CBE Ignited approach is to inspire a new generation of leaders to begin transforming beyond a time-based system to a competency-based school where learners are engaged in a guaranteed, failure-free curriculum, with an individualized assessment plan to achieve competency and have an active voice in setting measurable goals for their future pathways to success.

The essential questions this chapter answers include the following.

- What are important factors for superintendents in a CBE system?
- What does the superintendent perspective look like in CBE?
- What does the district road map to CBE implementation look like?
- What are the takeaways from this chapter?

What Are Important Factors for Superintendents in a CBE System?

There are many proven pathways to creating an effective CBE school system. However, after thirty years of helping systems transition into successful CBE organizations, we feel that the CBE Ignited approach is supported by not only the most experience but the most sustained success over decades. CBE is more than moving from a time-based to a competency-based system. It requires each system to examine its readiness to move an entire system forward and then strategically move each element of CBE until the system is in place. This is then followed up with a commitment to continually improve each element of the paradigm shift until the results reflect the potential of every stakeholder group. Influential change leaders instinctively understand that sustainable systems will not occur by mandate. A successful leader for CBE understands the need for fundamental realignment of expectations and creates strategies, processes, and action steps needed to collectively move the entire system forward. A change leader recognizes that the new system may not work for every student in the same time frame and has a deep commitment to a multiyear improvement process. Transformational change begins with the superintendent and district leadership team (DLT). School board members must share a commitment to assemble a group of stakeholders, which includes community leaders, parents, and students, to create consensus around shared beliefs and commit to an unwavering vision for student-centered teaching and learning.

System change leaders realize that simply tinkering with the current system will never achieve the desired results. Adopting a new literacy program or adjusting the daily class schedule will rarely accomplish the goal of ensuring academic success for all students. Change leaders are tenacious and relentless, regardless of the challenges and barriers they may face, and they will often put their education career on the line to do the right thing.

Successful district and school leaders earn the trust of their staff and community by engaging everyone in their shared vision for building a better education system that responds to the needs of all students. Advocates for CBE are also strong managers in that they can keep the district functioning at a high level during the challenges of a restructuring process. Courage involves pushing the envelope of innovation and embracing the chaotic surprises, while fully expecting it will often get messy before it gets better.

CBE leaders roll up their sleeves to be active learners in this journey. "Whatever it takes" is often a theme in these model schools and districts. The first to recognize the potential value of CBE are reliable and true servant-style leaders, in that they give credit to everyone when things are going well and take full responsibility when they do not. They inspire by action, but they recognize that passion is not always enough to succeed. These rare leaders collectively define success in terms of clear goals driven by a shared vision of developing a responsive road map with measurable outcomes. In the early adoption of CBE in high-performing schools since the 1990s, the leaders who focused on inclusion, high expectations, individualized student learning strategies, and continuous improvement found the greatest success.

The superintendent or CEO must be committed to leading the CBE journey. Many districts have inspired principals or teachers who are interested in exploring CBE at the school or classroom level. Because this is a transformative change, it requires a common vision and support from the executive leadership and the school board to succeed. Pockets of excellence are evident in every district, but in our experience, without districtwide support, visionary principals and classroom teachers often experience frustration or burnout and relocate to a district with a firmly established CBE model of instructional delivery. Here we discuss the necessary leadership characteristics that superintendents must exhibit, as well as considerations for change.

Leadership Characteristics

District and school leaders have all experienced the daunting task of first maintaining a functional organization while also navigating the challenges of the downstream impacts of the COVID-19 pandemic on student achievement. The pandemic caused school performance to suffer systemically because classrooms disappeared (MacGillis, 2023). Teachers were asked to revamp overnight to adopt new strategies for content delivery and the computer-screen-only method of class instruction. Many professionals thrived within the challenge; others were confused and often paralyzed by the antiquated, time-based requirements and testing prompts of the classroom that were never designed to engage a student sitting at a computer at home.

Lessons learned during the pandemic by all stakeholders have created a unique launching pad for innovation and substantive systems change. Teachers, parents, and students all experienced the unique opportunity for learning anytime and anywhere through a full menu of remote learning platforms and using new and exciting digital devices often offered to parents and students working remotely during the pandemic. Leaders who have the will to seize this global challenge to create innovative educational opportunities for their students can build on this once-in-a-lifetime seismic shift. This new expectation from learners, initially forced by makeshift remote learning mandates, fully embraces the future promise and potential of CBE. Leaders who are ready to embark on the CBE journey will possess many of the skills and dispositions outlined in the following chart (figure 6.1, page 142).

Considerations for Change

District and school leaders make hundreds of decisions every day just to maintain operations and educational programs. When it comes to changing any aspect of the current system, it is critical to understand the dynamics of any change process. Disrupting the status quo is a witch's cauldron of possible calamities, and initial reluctance on the part of any potential stakeholder must be expected. How do we discuss new ideas with our partners? Where do we find the keys to unlocking cooperation? Are there always winners and losers in a debate about what to do with our students? Are some methods and timelines to initiate change better than others? Is the initiative considered a first- or second-order change?

The short take on dealing with change in education is to gauge the commitment and scale of the proposed effort. Michael Fullan (2003) talks about first-order and second-order change in his book *Change Forces With a Vengeance*. Here are some of the characteristics of each of these changes, along with Richard's conception of an additional type, third-order change, to assist with determining what type of strategies will be needed and the potential realistic results of both pathways.

Characteristics of CBE Executive Leaders

Values and Beliefs	
Traditional System Commit to do the best within the current system.	**CBE System** ✓ Recognize the current system needs a major overhaul and are risk takers, committed to systems change through innovation.
Visioning Process	
Traditional System Follow a traditional strategic plan with mission and vision statements developed with the leadership team and school board, and periodically monitor progress on strategic objectives.	**CBE System** ✓ Include all stakeholders in the examination of the current student and school district performance by reviewing the performance data and studying characteristics of high-performing systems, and then challenge stakeholders to reimagine what schools could be. The strategic goals and objectives developed from this process are continually reviewed, monitored, and adjusted.
School Culture and Work Environment	
Traditional System Recognize the importance of a healthy workplace and culture of collaboration but are often reactionary in improving the culture.	**CBE System** ✓ Strategically create a positive collaborative work environment, based on respect and relationships. Understand the elements of a positive and safe school culture for all and effectively monitor and adjust as needed.
Management Style	
Traditional System Use a mostly top-down style, with some shared decision making, characterized by faculty committees and release time for teacher collaboration.	**CBE System** ✓ Exhibit willingness to make difficult decisions and understand the value of inclusive and collaborative input in critical decisions impacting student outcomes. Build on others' capacity to lead and share the leadership role.
Change Agent	
Traditional System Focus on maintaining a viable traditional system with incremental changes to improve teaching and learning. Employ new technologies and communication tools to operate the system within the status quo.	**CBE System** ✓ Relentlessly pursue the best system for all students and commit to continual learning and professional development for staff to build skills to navigate second-order change. Continually explore the integration of technology to support the work of all students, staff, and administration.
School District Leader	
Traditional System Facilitate focused discussions with school board members, encouraging them as ambassadors of the district to support incremental changes to improve student learning and provide the resources necessary to preserve programs in the current system.	**CBE System** ✓ Have a unique skill set that begins with working with the school board, asking the difficult questions, and inspiring others to respond to the collective vision. Driven by strong educational values and beliefs, and the recognition that every student has a unique pathway and the system has a responsibility to guide and support them.

Figure 6.1: Characteristics of CBE executive leaders.

First-Order Change

Some changes are easy and quick, while others take years to formulate a new culture for success. For example, if a state mandates a new high-stakes assessment protocol, then leaders will strategically communicate to stakeholders why and how the changes will take place. The new requirements may require the schools to quickly create after-school tutoring sessions or a handbook for students and parents on test-taking strategies. This response initiative is considered first-order or incremental change. *First-order change* is doing more or less of something you are likely already doing. It is nearly always reversible and nonthreatening.

The focus in an average district at most strategy sessions is spent on the year-end data representing student achievement scores, which depends on the present state of teacher training, aptitude, workspace, and student body dynamics and is not always sustainable. These strategies are usually incremental improvements that can easily be removed or altered with new leadership or dissension (adopting a new literacy program or class schedule, minor adjustments to policies or procedures, approving a strategic plan, and so on). What is missing by embracing small steps toward a goal is moral purpose, passion, commitment, and shared vision. This tweaking of the existing system is where most of the school improvement initiatives are presently active in schools because the risk factor to the entire system is low.

Educational researchers have cited their specific perspectives on first- and second-order change, including Robert J. Marzano, Timothy Waters, and Brian A. McNulty (2005), who have identified key characteristics that leaders need in these three different change cycles. The following leadership characteristics are expanded and prioritized in order of importance for the CBE change journey.

Leadership for first-order change requires the following.

- Emphasize relationships.
- Create a culture of collaboration.
- Establish strong lines of communication.
- Advocate for the school.
- Provide resources.
- Maintain visibility.
- Protect teachers from distractions.
- Look for and celebrate success.

Second-Order Change

Second-order change is either reacting to fundamental elements such as inadequate funding or population surprises or, more likely, being forced by political accountability or community activism to do something significantly or fundamentally different from what you have done before. The stakes are elevated, and the chance of complete failure waits in the wings for a misstep. These changes are never predictable or have full support of all concerned. If a local decision is made to go from a nine-month calendar to year-round schools, for example, the leader's strategies and communication challenges escalate compared to a first-order change and will change the status quo dramatically. A formidable reluctance to large-scale upheaval of the educational delivery model will generate strong pockets of resistance and debate.

The focus in a high-performing district is on systemic fundamental change that will unleash potential and commitment and gain easily measured positive results. These changes accomplish things never done before in this district and are proven to be sustainable in districts of similar community attributes (moving from a time-based to competency-based system; moving from scholastic credit and experience in your teacher pay structure to a structure that rewards performance and collaboration; adopting flipped classrooms throughout the district; measuring system success with close attention to keeping all students involved daily in pursuing their lifelong educational goals; and so on). These types of system change are difficult to reverse, if done correctly, and are driven by shared values and beliefs around learning that are fiercely protected by the stakeholders. Second-order change impacts the tenets and culture of an organization. This risk factor increases exponentially when building a structure for success, but the results can be life changing for entire communities if allowed to grow and bloom.

Leadership for second-order change requires the following.

- Operate from strong shared beliefs.
- Implement research and theory exploration.
- Propose new ideas.
- Develop a shared vision based on agreed beliefs.
- Create explicit goals for change.
- Define success in terms of specific goals.
- Embrace ambiguity and dissent.
- Expect things to seem worse in the beginning.

Third-Order Change

We must work beyond second-order change. Richard, working from Fullan's (2003) notion of first- and second-order change, developed the term *third-order change*. In short, third-order change occurs when the change itself creates a new culture that is easily scalable. Our crusade should be to focus our efforts on scaling up the second-order change in our schools, resulting in an exciting new paradigm that has the potential to go viral. Positive exposure of this potential game-changer may well result in a fundamental cultural shift regarding how the traditional classroom fits into a student's life learning goals. Examples of greater cultural third-order changes include iPhones, which started a revolution in how people access information and media, and Google Maps, which fundamentally changed the way we navigate on the road because of real-time data, alternate routes, and so on. An educational third-order change example in the evolving Russian system is its commitment to CBE (described on page 39), in which Richard played a critical role in advising a committed executive team. If you were to look into a typical Russian classroom, at best you would see a very traditional learning environment where the teacher is mainly operating from a lecture format with minimal engagement from the students: rote learning of facts and algorithms with no connection to their relevancy in the students' lives. However, in the personalized model in Russian schools, many aspects of the CBE model are evident, and engagement, rigor, and relevance take on a more critical role. This order of change is the gold ring, always sought after but rarely achieved, and takes years of passion and hard work to scale for success, but it can be a positive game-changer for schools, society, the workforce, and, most of all, each of our students.

The requirements for third-order change leadership derive from Richard's experience of decades of leading and supporting successful CBE systems. These are the characteristics that these organizations have adopted to remain sustainable, and they continue to produce positive results and are willing to help others on their CBE journey. Leadership for third-order change requires the following.

- Create a sustained culture of innovation driven by the shared vision.
- Attract like-minded individuals and empower them.
- Create a systemic leadership culture.
- Continually innovate and monitor trend data in all areas sustained over years.
- Document and tell your story and commit to help others on their journey.
- Create and monitor a clear road map of your multiyear journey.
- Utilize technology to implement, report, monitor, and improve your system.

The Change Process

It is important to understand that not everyone will be interested or ready for change. This is why, especially in second-order change, developing a focused and shared vision driven by the underlying beliefs and values of all the stakeholders is key. Often systemic failure of a school or district provides the leverage needed. The trail to the transition of an entire organization into a new set of rules and expectations requires at least 80 percent of stakeholders committed to instituting the change. A majority of staff is simply never enough. New ideas shaping such a traditional workplace are fragile and beautiful creatures, and their life expectancy is precariously short. Commitment means not just believing this is the right thing to do and holding on fast. In some cases, these high-level changes to the current practices require that teaching demands an upgrade to instructional methods, and each teacher and administrator will be held accountable for achieving the heavily questioned new standards. This is the biggest reason second-order change is difficult to sustain without discomfort to some of the stakeholders. Recall the three types of people that leaders encounter in organizations: (1) omnivores, (2) Missouri-ites, and (3) naysayers (see chapter 5, page 113).

Before the change process begins, it is important to have all three groups participate and allow ample opportunity to have all their disparate voices heard. It is also important as a change leader to protect the early adopters of the effort from undeserved criticism as the concept takes hold. Communication and leadership are the twin towers that allow change to happen in the face of fierce opposition.

These are important attributes for any district leader and manager, but effective CBE leaders need additional change leadership skills. In most instances, they are sequential from first- to second-order change, but there are times when it is possible to jump ahead right into second order. For example, perhaps a district has already adopted CBE, or a charter management organization such as Summit Schools (https://summitps.org) in California and Washington has already moved toward a personal proficiency system. This type of high-profile success story builds confidence for other regional change agents.

What Does the Superintendent Perspective Look Like in CBE?

As district leaders, superintendents make difficult decisions every day and are often overwhelmed with the multiple responsibilities of running a complex organization. In leading a CBE transition, your role will definitely change in comparison to just running a traditional district. Leaders who have had success in promoting first-order change are much more likely to be successful in leading second-order change. The core skills of building and maintaining relationships, trust, transparency, and effective communication are prerequisites in developing any successful second-order change. The inherent nature of moving from a time-based to a competency-based system creates new challenges not found in first-order change. The key among these are overhauling staff and student policies, scheduling, grading, eligibility, graduation requirements, curriculum, evaluations, and hiring practices, to name just a few. We refer to this journey as designing the airplane while you are busy flying it. One of the biggest challenges when you are ready to move into this new paradigm is maintaining a dual system until 100 percent of your schools have made the necessary transitions. One strategy is providing a waiver or grant permission from your school board to your innovative, early adaptive schools to allow adequate time to transition to the new system.

The superintendent, along with other key leaders, must be fully and personally engaged in driving this initiative for it to be successful. Without diligent executive support, the journey will begin to falter with the lack of continual attention to this restructuring. The superintendent or CEO must be fully committed to doing the heavy lifting of leading the change each and every day. This means attending all the trainings and being vulnerable to hard questioning from stakeholders. No one in charge has all the answers. Learn the strength of having shared big-picture questions with your team and learn together what answers will work for your specific issues. Leading by example is what inspires people and is a key trait for anyone considering this endeavor. In the following narrative, the journey begins in an urban district.

> *Superintendent Harding is the leader of an urban district of thirty thousand students with strong community support and a reputation for achieving excellence. The district is located in an area bordering Silicon Valley, California, with a strong economy based on high-paying jobs. The district receives statewide accolades for high achievement test scores and, because of the community profile, there is the perception that many of the graduates will attend prestigious universities. In this well-established traditional public school system, students move through classes competing for grades with a focus on achieving a high grade-point average. There is strong parental pressure on the students and teachers to prepare students for admission to top-tier colleges.*
>
> *Dr. Harding initially met with students, teachers, and faculty to discuss critical questions about student engagement and success. He worked with the directors of learning and assessment and the DLT to disaggregate student achievement data and graduation rates.*

The superintendent and DLT found that 20 percent of their ninth-grade students never reached high school graduation, which was an enviable high graduation rate for their state, but they knew they could do better by their students. The district prided itself on the statistic that 80 percent of the graduates went on to postsecondary studies; however, an examination of a graduate survey indicated that only 40 percent of the students made it past their second year in college.

After interviewing college graduates and reviewing survey results, it was clear that many students were ultimately successful in their careers but felt that high school was more of a social experience, and they played the game prescribed by their teachers to get good grades. They voiced that what they had learned in high school had little impact on their careers or provided relevance to the skills they needed in the workplace. The superintendent and leadership team were unsettled and concerned by what the data and downstream interviews revealed about their programs. District leaders were also unsure about what to do with this information, mainly because their schools appeared to be at the top of most measurements used by the state to target low-performing schools, but the reality of their long-term success revealed an entirely different picture.

Dr. Harding discussed these findings with several school board members and community leaders and decided to explore options for increasing long-term student success, retention rates on dropouts, and postsecondary outcomes for all students by taking a team of stakeholders, including students, to a conference concerning innovations in education. The team members listened to many of the established alternatives that were promoted for school improvement over the years, such as the integration of technology, project-based learning, and teaching 21st century skills. It wasn't until the group attended a breakout session called "Unleashing the Potential of Every Child in a CBE System" that interest sparked. What the team found unique about this timely presentation was that the presenter, after explaining the fundamental components of a CBE system, turned over the presentation to the students in their program.

The students shared their personal and diverse explorations of learning in a CBE culture. These presenters were a racial mix of students from low socioeconomic neighborhoods, and yet their presentation was inspiring. They each had an inner confidence, pride in their accomplishments, and hopeful dreams about their future and how this system actually delivered on its promise. All student presenters displayed total ownership in their learning path; it was never about the grades but exclusively about finding their future path in life and developing those skills that they would need. The students shared their personal struggles in the traditional school system and how this new system not only supported them but made learning meaningful and relevant. They described the culture of the schools and how students arrived early and stayed late because it was a safe and supportive learning environment that nurtured their goals without the coercive need of potential failure to drive any improvement. The learning targets were clear and scaffolded from simple to challenging with multiple ways of learning new information, culminating in a meaningful project or demonstration for an authentic audience. Projects were complex, exciting, inclusive, and connected to multiple subjects and were clearly and creatively designed by the students themselves.

These students demonstrated repeatedly how technology was ubiquitous in the new learning environment and how they were encouraged to use their phones as tools for learning. In fact, they shared their personal digital dashboards, which was an application on their phones. Students could articulate their exact level of achievement in every subject area. They were encouraged to accelerate instead of being held back in any way by the pace of the teacher or other classmates. Finally, the entire class shared how they were able to bring their learning anywhere, anyplace, anytime, and take more student ownership of how they wanted to demonstrate what they accomplished instead of passing an arbitrary test or assessment that had little personal significance and failed to plumb the depth and truth of their competency in any meaningful way.

Following the session, Dr. Harding and the team met with the presenter students and were impressed with their insights on their own learning strategies and the enthusiastic display of authentic passion for new and useful knowledge. The superintendent and leadership team left the conference with a new vision for learning and believed that CBE could make a difference for the district and student outcomes, but they were not sure about how to proceed. One week after returning from the conference, the superintendent met with others from the event to boldly take the first step on the CBE journey by designing an information session for the district advisory council and school board. This group of students and teachers shared the video of students from the CBE school telling their individual stories of accomplishment at the breakout session. It was the beginning. The journey of student-led excellence without failure had left the station and was steaming down the tracks toward student-engineered success.

The following narrative conveys the journey of a rural district.

> *One year after leading a small, rural school district, Superintendent Robbins engaged the DLT of principals, central office executives, and teacher leaders to develop a vision for improving success for a rapidly changing student demographic by focusing on individual student needs, both academic and emotional. The DLT understood that promoting transformative change would be challenging because the district was highly regarded and supported by the community and parents for the above-average student achievement results, successful athletics, and student participation in activities programs. The burning platform to support change was not as obvious as that in underperforming districts; however, despite the district's well-publicized success stories, many students were struggling academically and emotionally, due in large part to the socioeconomic disparities in the community and influence of drug and alcohol abuse throughout the region.*
>
> *Members of the DLT gathered additional student performance data by conducting focus groups, conducting surveys, and interviewing recent graduates and developed a report of findings, which was shared with multiple stakeholder groups. Using the results of a change readiness survey, the superintendent engaged CBE Ignited to meet with a comprehensive stakeholder group, including community and student leaders, to develop a vision statement and future-focused strategies. The student-centered vision for personal success propelled the district on a customized student planning and competency-based journey in partnership with the community that resulted in higher performance and student success.*

It is critically important that all stakeholders are invited to the table to be a part of this process. In a large district, this can be challenging logistically, but making the effort from the very beginning will pay off down the road. The vision must be created, driven, and improved on with the people it will impact the most. If you decide, as a school superintendent, to lead this change, it will likely be the most difficult journey in your professional career. Leaders who have *deployed the CBE playbooks with fidelity will have the single biggest impact on the lives and future success of everyone in their school community, most importantly their students.*

What are the critical roles that successful superintendents or CEOs have adopted in successfully managing this process? See figure 6.2.

Servant Leadership	Positive Relationships	Deep Learning	Readiness for Change	Shared Vision
1	2	3	4	5
Modeling	**Communication**	**Knowledge**	**Courage**	**Commitment**
First, understand your role, do your job exceedingly well, and always model servant leadership.	With all stakeholder groups, relationships and communications with board members are essential.	Commit yourself to deep learning about the change process as well as current trends on effective schools supported by research, especially concerning CBE.	Administer the CBE readiness survey or a similar screening tool to determine current levels of readiness for change. Communicate effectively and be transparent about your thinking.	Commit to training by being present and modeling that you are a learner as well. Create a shared vision and culture of collaboration with all staff and stakeholders to establish a preferred future and climate of cooperation that supports CBE.

Road Map Creation	Roles and Responsibilities	Deployment	Continuous Improvement	Storytelling
6	7	8	9	10
Priorities	**Empowerment**	**Engagement**	**Celebration**	**Mentorship**
Create, prioritize, and implement the critical steps on the road map moving toward a student-centered competency model or CBE.	Determine the roles and responsibilities of staff and stakeholder groups to support the CBE road map and empower them to help make decisions.	Engage and empower the CBE leadership team to oversee the deployment of the road map with regular progress updates; adjust as needed.	Regularly celebrate successes and commit to continuous improvement of the system by asking the difficult questions. Determine how to retain, recruit, train, and promote future staff that support CBE.	How will you tell your district's story? Be willing to help others on their journey.

Figure 6.2: Ten successful CBE leader characteristics.

Situational Deployment

When changing traditional schools to CBE, it is important to understand that we are trying to change a system fossilized in tradition. Every aspect of schools has been cemented and forged over centuries, so overcoming this inertia can be a long, slow process, and most change for those espousing the effort seems to move at a glacial rate.

Successful leaders don't just jump unprepared into this journey and mandate the changes simply because they have the position of authority. Effective leaders are cautious and strategic in understanding and exploring every aspect surrounding change and then commit themselves to understanding all aspects of CBE. True leaders determine what decisions they need to make alone and what ones should be jointly made. There will always be competing forces driving crucial decisions when leading this type of change. Learn to value the input of staunch critics as an essential guardrail for directing communitywide change.

Once you have begun the initial process and established positive momentum surrounding CBE, the district and school leaders can be much more direct and confident about making the decisions to sustain and improve the implementation of CBE. One of the tools we have embraced is called situational deployment. *Situational deployment* gives leaders a critical view of how to implement certain elements of CBE. Depending on the situation, we want to either involve everyone in the decision or simply give it to them and ask them to give their input. In the beginning of any change, you want an organic process where everyone's voice is valued, logged, and heard. Depending on the time you have and the extent of ownership you want your stakeholders to achieve, CBE can be facilitated in three different ways. Approach 1 suggests the fastest speed with very little ownership, while approach 3 implies you will get the highest rate of ownership with much time invested. We want stakeholders to experience the entire process using approach 3 (see figure 6.3). This tool organizes how we might deploy new ideas, such as a shared vision of competency, and gives us a framework on how to deploy this initiative. Later in the process, when revisiting the shared vision, you can use other approaches that either reinforce decisions that have already been made or re-energize a previous initiative to highlight an area of consensus.

Figure 6.4 (page 154) gives another visual representation of the change process.

System Change Versus Individual Change

The entire system needs to embrace this vision. The loftiest goals are not effective or sustainable otherwise. School leaders often initiate the foundations of system change with a handful of teachers who are eager and ready. There have been many examples of dedicated teachers who have started this movement within their individual classrooms. They were committed, passionate, and very competent in creating this new paradigm within their locus of control. For that single year of school, their students

Speed Versus Ownership		
Approach 1 **Give it to them completed** 	Approach 2 **Give it to them partially completed** 	Approach 3 **Have them create it and you facilitate** 
Very fast, little ownership	*Fast, some ownership*	*Slow, high ownership*
• Leader provides already made shared vision and code of collaboration. • Leader makes a presentation on every component of CBE with little or no participation from the stakeholders. • Leader provides all the materials: road maps, standard operating procedures, and so on.	• Leader provides partially completed shared vision and code of collaboration, while the other parts are done by the stakeholders. • Leader makes a presentation on every component of CBE with discussions from the stakeholders. • Leader provides some of the materials: road maps, standard operating procedures, and so on.	• Leader facilitates the process to create a shared vision and a code of collaboration. • Stakeholders go through activities and simulations to discover every component of CBE. Leader supports them if help is needed. • Stakeholders make materials themselves, while the leader provides examples (road maps, standard operating procedures, and so on).

Figure 6.3: CBE situational deployment for leaders.

experienced something that would give them confidence to challenge themselves to strive for competency. However, when these students moved on to a new classroom the following year, with a teacher not prepared to meet their individual needs, students may have become reluctant to return to sit-and-get timed delivery of material. It is likely that the process to return to a high-stakes testing protocol turns into frustration, and the student may quickly revert back to being a passive learner. The entire system needs to gain momentum and critical mass to finally move collectively into this new vision. We have learned that our best chance to scale this movement to a

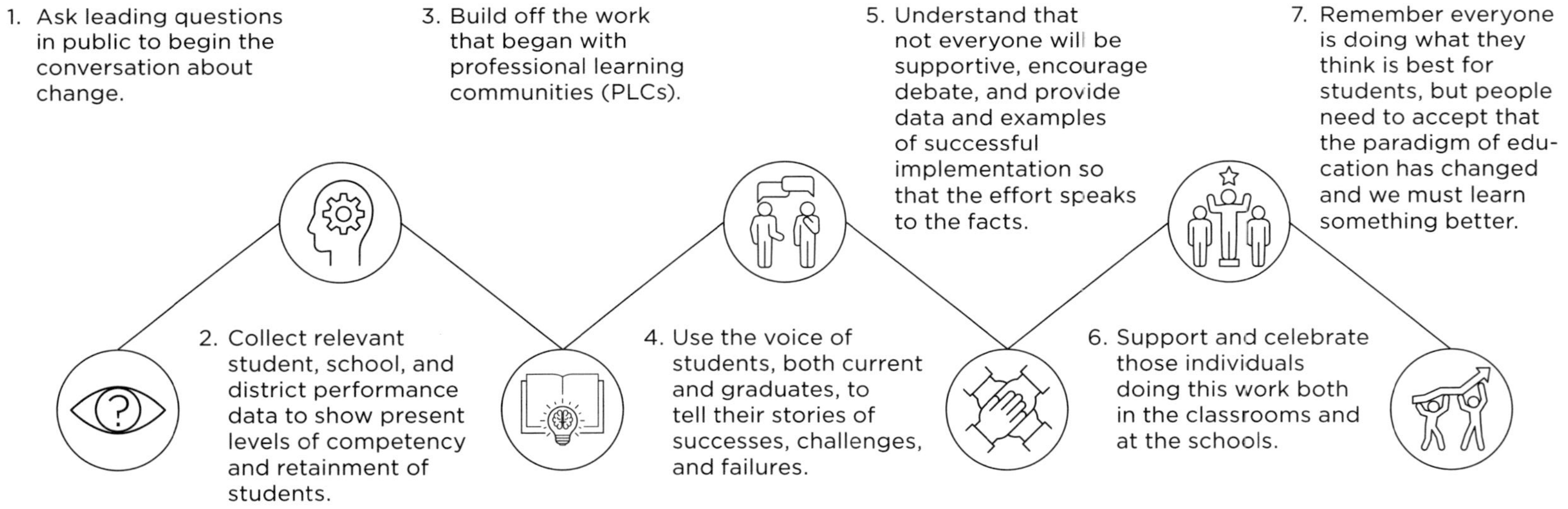

Figure 6.4: The art of addressing change.

greater playing field is to work within the whole system through modeling and a sharp focus on student data to demonstrate the value of CBE across the board. Only when a majority of practitioners and students report success without failure does the local experiment have the chance to become sustainable, replicable, and scalable.

Other CBE Opportunities: Charter Schools, Alternative Schools, and Schools Within a School

In a charter school environment, the dynamics are different. The school leaders have already established the culture and vision. As a result, parents and students are making their choice to attend this school because the school's vision aligns closely with their philosophy. In selecting a CBE charter school, parents have reviewed the available options and choose to send their child to a school where students are in charge of their own learning and are deeply engaged in meaningful work that will prepare them for their future in a powerful way.

A charter school principal generally has more autonomy and flexibility than a traditional school principal, who is governed by a larger district and the bureaucracy that follows. It is assumed that charter management organizations, which are set up to manage many charter schools, will continue to play a big role in pressuring traditional districts to change.

As more research comes to light that our schools are failing, and specifically our inability to meet the needs of all students to be successful in this global economy, there will be more opportunities to really shift our system to new and innovative models.

Every district has a handful of radical high-impact educators who have grown impatient with the status quo. Sometimes the teachers who want to change the paradigm by themselves create alternative programs within existing schools. These courageous teachers, due to their ongoing success with all students, are often given the autonomy to create a school within a school. Initially, other staff members see them as nonthreatening to the status quo and believe that what these outliers from tradition are doing will make their jobs easier because noncompliant and unengaged students will gravitate to these alternative programs, making the traditional teacher's job more manageable without those high-need students. These one-room alternative schools, or even a select team of teachers who want to create something better for students, begin with a shared vision to help meet the needs of all students. This self-efficacy shift begins to build a positive reputation in the eyes of students and parents because they feel valued, own their learning opportunities, and may find meaning and self-discovery for the first time.

Students share their successes in CBE with their peers. A student-centered proficiency system doesn't waste time, and the teachers personalize the learning around how, when, and why a student learns best. The interest to participate in this type of learning environment increases with each successful student. Students embrace this type of schooling and soon become very vocal advocates for change. When this happens, the one-room school within a school may soon need ten classrooms to keep up with the demand. The alternative to traditional teaching now becomes a threat to the old school system, and a teacher morale issue within regular classrooms becomes a tangible liability. Traditional teachers find themselves losing high-performing students and blaming this alternative school for taking more and more of the traditional successful students. Ironically, in our experience, this eroding attrition rarely results in traditional teachers reflecting upon their own practices to increase learning.

Most start-up or pilot proficiency classrooms, including flipped classrooms and hybrid instructional methods, have failed to create the necessary momentum to change the entire system. These CBE experiments either wind up being pockets of excellence, working in isolation with the tepid support of the administration, or the teachers who began the new model leave to find a system more aligned to their best practices.

Successful charter schools, alternative schools, and schools within a school create important opportunities for learning, data collection, and replication by the traditional system. Providing opportunities for teachers, students, and parents to shadow the engaged students and visit CBE classrooms can be a powerful strategy to build interest in transforming the traditional system by learning from firsthand experiences of stakeholders in a successful new model.

What Does the District Road Map to CBE Implementation Look Like?

When moving education toward a CBE philosophy, there are many moving pieces happening at once. A committed CBE executive leader will need a quiver of tools and strategies to be successful. One of the critical pieces is to have the leadership team develop a district road map that guides the journey toward implementing CBE on a realistic timeline. There are many changes that need to occur simultaneously, including staff training, curriculum updates, adopting instructional strategies, developing learning targets, implementing new policies, and creating evaluation and feedback procedures. At times, it can be daunting. Fortunately, there are organizations and resources available, and other districts and schools to network with, that have already embarked on the journey. See appendix A (page 183) for more information.

The purpose of the road map is to provide a scope and sequence of events that are necessary to implement CBE at the district level. The CBE district road map provides insight into the different progression levels that each stakeholder needs to undertake. This is a progression of events over time that successful districts have adopted. Every district will look different depending on its unique situation and readiness level. Recall that besides the systemwide or district map that targets school leaders and policymakers, teachers will need to have their own road maps to expedite this transition (see chapter 4, page 73).

There are six stages to help guide the district leader in the journey from *information* to *replication*. The first stage begins when the superintendent and DLT members recognize the need to unleash the new protocols and expectations of staff and students, and the final stage after the system is up and highly functional is taking time to share, collaborate, and support new systems that are interested in this vision for learning. Following is a brief overview of each level in the ideal progression.

The final stage has been strategically added to help successful leaders assist and mentor others. This is how inspired and successful leaders can collectively help change the current education system. This call to arms means that once you have reached the final stage of your road map to student success, you will be writing, speaking, and eventually helping others on their journey.

A Worthy Investment

When there's no clear path forward toward a leader's goals, it's very easy for that leader to slip into a cycle of regret. During many of my large conference presentations for educational leaders, I have become discouraged when following my keynote only a handful of leaders actively take up the challenge to transform their system. My audience recognizes that their schools are continually failing to meet every student's needs, and the next steps call for a radical change in how we prepare our students for their future. My consolation is that a very small percentage do indeed take action. Classroom teachers, building principals, or superintendents attending these targeted presentations are the doers, the change agents, who will seize the moment and move ahead. I am always humbled by a doer's passion and dedication that flows in order to make this type of change a reality, for simply no other reason than it is the right thing to do. These are the pivotal game-changers that will carry the torch of CBE for generations to come.

In 2008, at an Effective Schools Conference sponsored by Larry Lezotte in Arizona, there were one thousand educators in attendance at my keynote. I had brought along several copies of my book *Delivering on the Promise: The Education Revolution* (DeLorenzo et al., 2008) to try and arm those who will lead us to the change we need with the results I had proven to be possible in the learning environment of the schools in Alaska and around the world. The presentation, in spite of my low expectations, elicited from the audience the excitement and level of engagement and commitment that I was hoping for. The energy in the room was electric. At the end of my session, I held my book up and offered it to anyone who thought they would like to lead this exciting journey in their own schools. I challenged each professional in the audience to meet me for more information at the bar and, for those who took the time, I would present them with my book and buy them a drink. All I asked in return is that I would love to see their own quick draft of a road map leading toward the next step in the process. In the past, I would usually get a couple of leaders who were both curious and genuinely interested in moving the conversation to the next level, but never more than a handful.

I should have heeded the old adage, "Be careful what you wish for." At this particular event, I arrived at the bar at 5:00 P.M. as promised, and to my surprise, there were 122 people waiting for me. I was blown away at the response. My bar tab for these can-do leaders came to $1,255.00. Thank God it was happy hour. In retrospect, it was one of the best investments I had ever made. Many of those committed activists have embraced the promise of CBE and gone on to lead their classes, schools, and districts in effecting change for their students. And I got a good story to share with more future educational leaders.

—RICHARD A. DELORENZO

The CBE road map is your guide to implementing all the elements of CBE in your system. We encourage districts to customize your self-assessment road map to match the characteristics of your situation. In fact, the process expects all staff members to have their personal road maps in place when the change begins because your roles can dramatically shift from bystander to active practitioner in the experiment that lies ahead, and this contract made with yourself will keep you on course. The progression stages of the district road map are the same as those for schools; see figure 5.3 (page123) for an overview. In the following series of figures, we will highlight each stage; then we will provide a sample district road map document.

In the first stage, information, the district has recognized that schools are not meeting the needs of all students, and key leaders are committed to learn more about CBE and conduct a team visit to observe a CBE school. There is an awareness level of CBE by the school board, and high interest from the DLT to proceed. There is no commitment at this point. See figure 6.5.

In the awareness stage, there is a commitment from the DLT to deep dive into evaluating the next steps for adopting the CBE model. One of the initial elements that will help determine a school system's potential to adopt a CBE system is to complete the CBE readiness survey (see chapter 5, page 113, for a sampling of questions).

There are some critical elements that can either hinder or accelerate the journey. Here are some of those items that determine an organization's readiness to move quickly toward CBE.

- Trust between different stakeholder groups
    - What is the trust level between central administration and schools, principals and teachers, and teachers and students?
    - What is the attrition rate of staff and students?

Awareness

Am I ready to move our education system toward the future?

- What are your values and beliefs around learning?
- How does your current system align to your values and beliefs? For example, do your students learn at different rates, are all your students' needs being met (delayed or accelerated in learning), and are all students actively engaged in learning?
- How does your current system align to the values and beliefs of CBE?
- Why do schools need to change?
- What is the burning platform or opportunity?
- What would the new system look like if it was aligned to your values and beliefs?
- What should a day in the life of a CBE learner look like?

Awareness → **Readiness** → **First Implementation** → Routine → Refinement → Replication

Next Steps:

- Follow up with CBE Ignited team and coach.
- Speak with other districts who have done this and hear about their successes and challenges.
- Share ideas with your leadership team.

Figure 6.5: CBE road map for superintendents—Awareness.

- Effective communication between different stakeholder groups
  - What are the processes used to communicate?
  - What are some current initiatives in the district?
  - How were those movements shared with others?
- Level of trust and collaboration between stakeholder groups
  - What is the collegial climate like in each school?
  - What is the relationship and communication between district administrators and staff?
- Effectiveness of key leaders
  - What have been the key goals and initiatives for recent improvement initiatives, and what progress has been made in addressing the problem?
  - What do the trend data reveal about the success of past initiatives?
- School board leadership and effectiveness
  - Is the board committed to supporting and providing the resources to support new initiatives to improve student results?
  - What are the relationships and communication styles among board members and administration, teachers, students, and parents?
- Extent to which school or district is driven by results
  - Are targeted schools safe?
  - How do you define and measure long-term success?
  - What is the ongoing vision evolving for the district and schools, and how is this essential process measured?
  - What are the strengths and challenges of accomplishing your long-range vision?

A feedback report is prepared and provided to the leadership team to determine readiness to proceed with the next level. The report will highlight and provide a guide for additional attention that might be needed to address specific stakeholder concerns and develop a strategy to mitigate fundamental disagreements in advance. If there is a positive report in all areas, then there is an excellent chance of being successful in implementing the next level of CBE or moving into an implementation phase. However, if there are major issues surrounding trust, collaboration, and effectiveness of the road map, it becomes much more difficult to adopt CBE. Often, those districts that fall short of systemic support initially spend some targeted remedial planning time and invite suggestions for working toward addressing those key connective areas internally before having another readiness survey conducted.

When visiting education systems to ascertain their readiness, there often seem to be two opposing forces at work: (1) the perceived readiness by the leadership team and (2) stakeholder groups facing the reality of a major upheaval of student learning and assessment practices. Often the perception and reality are in perfect alignment, but many times they are not, which creates difficult obstacles in moving forward. Going slowly with a clear message and plan to bring together strategy and reality helps change agents identify where they can move faster toward building a clearly defined path toward success for every student. Prepare for staying the course for change is what we advise organizations to consider. The purpose of the CBE readiness survey is to help leaders understand exactly what their current level of readiness to tackle this effort looks like.

Once leaders have deployed and analyzed the CBE readiness survey, they can develop a district CBE road map and move on to readiness. Figure 6.6 (page 162) provides an overview of the readiness stage of the road map.

The superintendent, with endorsement of the school board and commitment from the DLT, decides to move forward. This is the first implementation stage. A shared vision and code of collaboration for CBE has been developed with district stakeholders. The district adopts a comprehensive CBE road map, and has at least 10 percent of the staff and 100 percent of the administration ready to be trained in CBE. Roles and responsibilities of all stakeholder groups have been clearly defined. See figure 6.7 (page 163).

In the routine stage, progress can be documented in each area of the CBE road map. There is a commitment of at least 80 percent of the teachers who are ready to implement CBE in classrooms. The shared vision and road map have been communicated with all the stakeholders. See figure 6.8 (page 164).

In the refine stage, 100 percent of staff are committed and actively practicing CBE in their schools and classrooms. Processes are now being refined based on data. A CBE culture has been established and continues to improve in all areas. See figure 6.9 (page 165).

The replication stage is characterized by reaching the refinement stage in each area. There are multiple years of positive data and clear processes to sustain CBE in the system. CBE leaders are willing to help other teachers, principals, and superintendents in this journey. See figure 6.10 (page 166).

Figure 6.11 (page 167) shows what a district road map document looks like.

Readiness

Is my district ready for change and open to new ideas of what education looks like, feels like, and acts like?

- Do we have safe schools and a culture of acceptance?
- Do we have quality teachers in every classroom?
- Do we have a guaranteed and viable curriculum?
- Do we have the right curriculum for our students' future?
- Are all our students, teachers, and administrators committed to creating effective schools?
- How will we build leadership capacity?
- Do we have the capacity to transition to a CBE system?
- What are our strengths and barriers of moving toward CBE?
- What can we learn from other districts implementing CBE?
- What will our CBE road map look like?

Awareness → **Readiness** → **First Implementation** → Routine → Refinement → Replication

Next Steps:

- Have the DLT participate in CBE training.
- Self-assess your readiness.
- Create a road map and prioritize steps to support CBE in your district.

Figure 6.6: CBE road map for superintendents—Readiness.

First Implementation

Does our DLT have a dedicated team to coordinate outside support services and lead the communication, feedback, and reporting of results to all stakeholders?

- Who will be the point person or team to lead this transition?
- What will our initial CBE road map look like?
- How will we schedule the training necessary for all stakeholders?
- What are the internal and external barriers of moving toward CBE?
- How will CBE impact our policies, financials, human resources, curriculum, digital platform, and assessment practices?

Next Steps:

- DLT has 80 percent of all staff committed to adopt CBE.
- DLT supports principals and SLTs by providing training and support in recruiting faculty and promoting teacher leaders.
- DLT develops scope and sequence of learning targets with scales, assessments, instructional strategies, and reporting documents supporting best practices.

Figure 6.7: CBE road map for superintendents—First implementation.

Routine

Do we have 80 percent or more of the total stakeholders supporting the system change to CBE?

- What is our plan to address our policies, financials, human resources, digital platform, curriculum, and assessment practices?
- What is the current progress on our CBE road map?
- What are our results in regard to our vision, road map, and barriers of moving toward CBE?
- How should we collect our data and processes to tell our story?
- What should our leadership system look like to sustain CBE?

Awareness → **Readiness** → **First Implementation** → **Routine** → Refinement → Replication

Next Steps:

- DLT determines what are the critical changes needed at the district, school, and classroom levels.
- DLT adopts a CBE digital platform and uploads all student data, curriculum, assessments, and so on.

Figure 6.8: CBE road map for superintendents—Routine.

Refinement

What are our processes for refining the scope and sequence of learning targets with scales, assessments, instructional strategies, and reporting documents based on results?

- How are we continually improving on our processes?
- What are the changes needed on our CBE road map?
- What do our trend data look like?
- Does our human resources system support CBE and include recruiting, training, evaluating, and promoting educators?
- How will we celebrate our current success?
- How will we tell our story?
- How will we provide support, coaching, and training to other schools outside our district?

Next Steps:

- Organize documents to be able to share your story.

Figure 6.9: CBE road map for superintendents—Refinement.

Replication

Are we ready to share our stories locally, regionally, and internationally?

- Do we have a compelling story to share?
- How many teachers and schools are implementing CBE with fidelity?
- How do we sustain our innovation and continued improvement?

Awareness → Readiness → First Implementation → Routine → Refinement → **Replication**

Next Steps:

- Utilize the LMS to review the shared vision, targets, and pacing.
- Create multiple ways to communicate progress and challenging areas including strategies for moving forward.
- Learn strategies for integrating social-emotional learning and the heart for each student.

Figure 6.10: CBE road map for superintendents—Replication.

Critical Questions	Tools and Strategies	Critical Components	Changes Needed	Timeline and Deliverables
Awareness Level *(This is before you commit.)*				
• What are your values and beliefs around learning? • How does your current system align to your values and beliefs? For example, do your students learn at different rates, are all your students' needs being met (delayed or accelerated in learning), and are all students actively engaged in learning? • How does your current system align to the values and beliefs of CBE? • Why do schools need to change? • What is the burning platform or opportunity? • What would the new system look like if it was aligned to your values and beliefs? • What should a day in the life of a CBE learner look like?	• What are the tools and strategies needed to transition to CBE *(parking lot, standard operating procedures, plus-delta, affinity diagram, power voting, root cause analysis, think-pair-share, Pareto chart, goal setting, commit-o-gram, T-chart)*?	• What are the critical components of CBE, and what does this look like in the district, school, and classroom *(values and beliefs toward learning, growth mindset, time-based versus competency-based systems, effective traditional teaching, shared vision, code of collaboration, learning targets with scales, effective instructional delivery, meaningful assessments and reporting of progress, digital platform)*?	• What changes will the district need to make to adopt CBE *(creating a guaranteed and viable curriculum, promotion of students, report card, honor roll, graduation requirements, situational grouping, students grading, acceleration of students, eligibility requirements, and so on)*? ▪ Policy at the local and state level ▪ Technical support—LMS ▪ Training support—face-to-face, hybrid, and virtual ▪ One-, three-, and five-year vision	• What is a realistic timeline to implement this with fidelity in our district? ▪ 10 percent of the schools ▪ 80 percent of the schools ▪ 100 percent of the schools • Deliverables: ▪ Schedule of meetings and minutes discussing awareness level topics

Figure 6.11: Sample district road map.

continued →

Critical Questions	Tools and Strategies	Critical Components	Changes Needed	Timeline and Deliverables
Readiness Level *(This is before you commit; leadership team is led by the superintendent or CEO.)*				
• Do we have safe schools and a culture of acceptance? • Do we have quality teachers in every classroom? • Do we have a guaranteed and viable curriculum? • Do we have the right curriculum for our students' future? • Are all our students, teachers, and administrators committed to creating effective schools? • How will we build leadership capacity? • Do we have the capacity to transition to a CBE system? • What are our strengths and barriers of moving toward CBE? • What can we learn from other districts implementing CBE? • What will our CBE road map look like?	• Leadership needs to understand first- and second-order change. • Leadership needs to understand how to use tools effectively to move toward more effective schools *(readiness survey, creating a district road map to include shared vision, code of collaboration, guaranteed and viable curriculum, effective teachers in every classroom, and so on)*. • Understand the tools and strategies necessary to move toward CBE *(parking lot, standard operating procedures, plus-delta, power voting, root cause analysis, think-pair-share, Pareto chart, goal setting, commit-o-gram, T-chart)*.	• Leadership team needs to reflect on their district, school, and classroom practices and determine their values around effective schools. • Leadership team needs to understand the difference between traditional schools and CBE schools. • Leadership team needs to share and develop strategies around a CBE readiness report (external agency) to determine their next steps to implement CBE *(trust level between groups, school board voting, attrition rate of all staff, community, union, and administrators' relations)*. • Leadership team needs to complete a gap analysis between current practices and CBE.	• Leadership team needs to understand changes in policies and procedures to support CBE *(human resources, curriculum related policies, teacher professional development, student policies, and adopting a digital platform)*. • Superintendent needs to communicate with all stakeholders, but especially the school board, throughout the process. • Leadership team designs a preliminary road map that unpacks the transition toward CBE.	• One to three months: ▪ Leadership team needs 100 percent of administrators and 10 percent of staff committed to training. • Deliverables: ▪ Create a DLT. ▪ Readiness survey ▪ Strategies developed and shared around district readiness report ▪ Mandatory leadership training for all administrators ▪ Gap analysis report ▪ Preliminary road map ▪ Board recommendation and support

Critical Questions	Tools and Strategies	Critical Components	Changes Needed	Timeline and Deliverables
First Implementation Level *(With external support, this is when early adopters try it out.)*				
• Who will be the point person or team to lead this transition? • What will our initial CBE road map look like? • How will we schedule the training necessary for all stakeholders? • What are the internal and external barriers of moving toward CBE? • How will CBE impact our policies, financials, human resources, curriculum, digital platform, and assessment practices?	• Leadership team needs to invite all stakeholders to understand the components of CBE. • Leadership team needs to create a process to determine the commitment level of teachers, administrators, students, parents, and others. • Leadership team is modeling the use of tools *(parking lot, standard operating procedures, plus-delta, power voting, root cause analysis, think-pair-share, Pareto chart, goal setting, commit-o-gram, effective meeting protocols)*.	• Leadership team needs to support the early adopters by providing professional development opportunities for all stakeholders. • District needs at least 10 percent of teachers and all administrators on board with CBE. • Leadership team needs to have a point person or a dedicated team to coordinate outside support services and lead the communication, feedback, and reporting of results to all stakeholders. • Digital platform to support CBE should be researched.	• Leadership team needs to determine what are the critical changes needed at the district, school, and classroom level *(human resources, curriculum-related policies, teacher professional development, student policies, and adopting a digital platform)*. • Leadership team needs a comprehensive road map that unpacks the transition toward CBE.	• Three to six months: ▪ Leadership team needs 80 percent of one school's staff committed to training. • Deliverables: • Establish a point person to lead CBE implementation • Implement a comprehensive road map to include transition to CBE.

continued →

Critical Questions	Tools and Strategies	Critical Components	Changes Needed	Timeline and Deliverables
Routine Level *(This is proof of concept; 80 percent of staff have committed to adopt CBE.)*				
• What is our plan to address our policies, financials, human resources, digital platform, curriculum, and assessment practices? • What is the current progress on our CBE road map? • What are our results in regard to our vision, road map, and barriers of moving toward CBE? • How should we collect our data and processes to tell our story? • What should our leadership system look like to sustain CBE?	• Leadership team needs to adopt or create a CBE district tool kit. • Leadership team needs to create a shared vision with all stakeholders. • Leadership team needs to adopt quality guidelines (for example, total quality management) to ensure that the vision, code of collaboration, and implementation of CBE is being monitored and adjusted.	• Leadership team needs 80 percent of all staff committed to adopt CBE. • Leadership team needs to support administrators by providing training and support recruiting and promoting new staff. • Leadership team needs to develop scope and sequence of learning targets with scales, assessments, instructional strategies, and reporting documents supporting best practices.	• Leadership team needs to implement the critical changes needed at the district, school, and classroom level. • Leadership team needs to either build or purchase a CBE digital platform and upload all student data, curriculum, assessments, and so on. • Leadership team needs to adopt policies to support CBE. ▪ Administrator training ▪ Curriculum-related policies ▪ Human resources procedures ▪ Teacher professional development ▪ Student policies	• Six to twelve months: ▪ Leadership team needs 80 percent of staff and at least 30 percent of the schools committed to training. • Deliverables: ▪ Revised road map ▪ Plan to address our policies, financials, human resources, digital platform, curriculum, and assessment practices

Critical Questions	Tools and Strategies	Critical Components	Changes Needed	Timeline and Deliverables
Refinement Level *(This is positive trend data in student, teacher, and administrative effectiveness.)*				
• How are we continually improving our processes? • What are the changes needed on our CBE road map? • What do our trend data look like? • Does our human resources system support CBE and include recruiting, training, evaluating, and promoting educators? • How will we celebrate our current success? • How will we tell our story? • How will we provide support, coaching, and training to other schools outside our district?	• Leadership team needs to refine its tools and process based on results and document its journey. • Leadership team needs to re-energize its shared vision and code of collaboration.	• Leadership team needs to refine its scope and sequence of learning targets with scales, assessments, instructional strategies, and reporting documents based on results.	• Leadership team needs to refine policies based on data. ▪ Administrator training ▪ Curriculum-related policies ▪ Human resources procedures ▪ Teacher professional development ▪ Student policies • Leadership team needs to document their journey by collecting all the tools, processes, and data that define their journey. • Leadership team needs to refine their induction and training to attract new educators. • Leadership team needs to create a leadership system to promote teacher and administrator advancement within and outside the system.	• One to three years: ▪ Leadership team needs 100 percent of staff and 100 percent of the schools committed to training. • Deliverables: ▪ Revised road map ▪ Revised policies and procedures ▪ Repository of our data to tell our story ▪ Comprehensive human resources system to support CBE to include classified, certified, and administration staff

continued →

Critical Questions	Tools and Strategies	Critical Components	Changes Needed	Timeline and Deliverables
Replication Level *(This is three years plus.)*				
• Do we have a compelling story to share? • How many teachers and schools are implementing CBE with fidelity? • How do we sustain our innovation and continued improvement?	• Leadership team needs to document their story from the lens of the students (learners), teachers (facilitators), parents, and administration.	• Leadership team needs to present their story locally, regionally, and nationally.	• Leadership team needs to share their story by opening their schools and district for others to visit.	• Three to five years • Deliverables: ▪ Leadership team needs to build a systematic recruitment cycle to certify, train, evaluate, and promote new educators.

What Are the Takeaways From This Chapter?

Leadership is where CBE begins, and the path forward for a school leader is a gauntlet of critical decisions. School district superintendents, often thought of as CEOs, especially in large districts or charter management organizations, are committed to implementing change and must possess a strong vision for and knowledge of CBE. Because we are in the beginning stages of CBE's potential, it will take courageous leaders, dedicated practitioners, and sound systemwide ownership of the process to achieve maximum results. There are currently several CBE leaders forging a path forward in schools throughout our country, and they are inspiring exciting change through their passion for student success. These catalysts for change are mission driven and totally committed to the personal success of every student in every classroom.

CHAPTER 7

A Vision for a New Future

The future of CBE looks hopeful, as this approach to learning focuses student success through the demonstration of skills and knowledge, rather than seat-time requirements and letter grades. With the pace of change in the modern world, both employers and the workforce must engage in lifelong learning to keep pace with and leverage new technologies, innovations, and practices. As a result, CBE and the clear demonstration of skills and evidence of competencies will become increasingly critical to students and employers. In addition, with increasing expansion and popularity of online learning resulting from the COVID-19 pandemic, CBE provides a flexible and convenient learning model, allowing students to learn at their own pace in their own way and on their own schedule. Institutions of higher education are in many ways ahead of the K–12 system because they are beginning to shift their efforts into a CBE philosophy in order to attract and retain students who will look elsewhere to gain invaluable knowledge, skills, and dispositions that guarantee economic mobility. Western Governors University (www.wgu.edu) is such a school that has embraced CBE at the postsecondary level.

The essential questions this chapter answers include the following.

- How will CBE be scaled to shift our educational system?
- What will CBE look like in the future?
- What are the takeaways from this chapter?

How Will CBE Be Scaled to Shift Our Educational System?

Bringing a new CBE vision of learning to scale takes an incredible groundswell of support. There needs to be a deep commitment from key stakeholders and policy leaders to embrace this type of change. This will take a well-coordinated effort at many levels. Everything from policy to teacher training will need to be overhauled in a concerted effort to bring about this new system. Unfortunately, at this time in the United States, we have not reached that critical mass of support. We have hundreds of schools that clearly illustrate what a CBE system looks like. These examples have sustained, positive results over years. However, until we reach a critical mass of schools embracing CBE by overcoming the inertia of the traditional education system, we will not see the full impact of this philosophy.

In our work, we have influenced and have established a proof of concept in many schools and districts, but unless we reach thousands of districts representing every conceivable demographic, we will continue to be mired in an antiquated system that allows only incremental improvements.

CBE will continue to grow because future economics will demand it. There is already a clear call to action from business leaders for schools and higher education institutions to prepare students with skills that they will need to thrive in their futures (Hall et al., 2023). The next step is to identify the visionary educational leaders who have the courage to transition to CBE in a variety of districts that represent the diversity and challenges found in the United States. Another option is a national or state movement that provides the freedom and incentive to innovate and embark on this journey, which allows them to move into this rarified air of CBE. Several states have already embarked on the journey by passing policies that allow for competency-based graduation and innovation districts that have flexibility with bureaucratic reporting requirements. The Aurora Institute (https://aurora-institute.org) identifies twenty-eight states leading the CBE journey and more taking the initial steps to provide enough flexibility at the district level to unleash a new system of accountability for student growth and learning outcomes (Gagnon, 2023). See appendix A (page 183) for a list of schools and districts that are implementing CBE.

Essential factors for scaling competency-based learning in the future include the following.

- **Leadership:** Sustaining and scaling CBE takes courageous leaders who will do whatever it takes to provide student-centered, customized learning for all students.
- **Vision:** Be clear about our collective vision for student success and learning.
- **Assessment and digital platform:** Change the way we measure student learning. Traditional grading systems that are based on seat time and standardized tests are not aligned with the goals of competency-based learning. Instead, we need to leverage new technologies, especially AI, and develop ways to measure, monitor, and record each student's progress on meeting competencies.

- **Student voice:** Put students at the center of the educational system by giving them a voice in their learning, and customize learning plans and opportunities to meet their unique needs and interests.
- **Professional development and coaching:** Provide teachers with the training and support they need. Competency-based learning requires teachers to have a different set of skills and knowledge than traditional teachers. This means providing faculty and staff with the training and support they need to implement competency-based learning effectively and giving them the time to make this transition.
- **Learning environment:** Rethink the role of the school. In a competency-based learning environment, the school is not just a place where students go to learn. It is also a place where students can go to get help with their learning, to collaborate with other learners, and to receive feedback from their peers and mentors.

Scaling CBE is the goal of this book, and to do this, we need leadership at the top to understand why this is a better way to educate all students and prepare them for their future as the current system fails to do. We have shared the CBE stories and road map to student success that our team paved in Chugach, Alaska, with many districts in the United States and around the world. Russia is the country that has made the greatest strides by embracing the vision for CBE and scaling this new educational system (Investment to the Future, n.d.a). Since 2017, the government, in partnership with leadership from the private sector, has taken extensive steps and made investments in education in order to keep pace with global competition. Some Russian leaders recognize the current education model is obsolete and have joined a consortium to bring about this innovative change, through teacher training and the creation of the next-generation CBE digital learning platform (Investment to the Future, n.d.b). At the peak of the Russian transformation to CBE prior to the invasion of Ukraine beginning in 2022, thousands of educators were being trained weekly in personalized learning, which is the term many Russian educators use for the concept of CBE (Investment to the Future, n.d.a).

The driving force in creating CBE schools was to give them a jump start into entering the global economy and become a leader in innovation and technology. Unless America can scale this vision with quality, CBE will follow in the footsteps of other so many other innovations that lose momentum and succumb to the latest trend in our classrooms. But if we can scale these concepts, it will provide future generations some hope.

What Will CBE Look Like in the Future?

CBE will transform the educational landscape in those districts, states, and nations that embrace a new vision for student-centered learning that is supported by teachers as facilitators of learning and fueled by a robust digital platform that manages customized student learning goals and progress. Because you are reading this book and exploring future options for student learning and success, you are a visionary leader who recognizes the failure of the current system to meet the needs of all students, and have already begun the process of learning about a new system. Fortunately, you are not alone, and there is a groundswell of interest, with hundreds of committed educators and policymakers who have taken the important first steps to transform systems and policies to support CBE.

The notion that a teacher will be standing in front of a room delivering the lecture format to a room full of students is obsolete. The one-size-fits-all learning model will be a thing of the past. We will understand complex algorithms and how to apply them in solving critical issues in a matter of minutes. Every aspect of our lives will be impacted by the increasing power of AI. Educators, industry leaders, and politicians will continue to wrestle with the challenges and opportunities inherent with the breakneck advancement of new technologies. Education has a track record of making slow and incremental changes and will continue to do so until visionary innovation leaders send a call for action to transform the education system by articulating compelling reasons to change and a clear pathway of how to get there.

Advancements in artificial intelligence are creating a watershed moment in learning. AI will be used to personalize learning unlike anything we have experienced by providing real-time feedback and customized recommendations on learning goals and strategies. Teachers will become facilitators in the future in that they will be required to collect, analyze, and prescribe personalized trajectories for each student. They will need to collaborate, problem solve, and continue to innovate to help each student succeed. Soon afterward, students will take on their learning pathways and will accelerate and be engaged in a much deeper way. This will continue throughout their lives and hopefully bring a much happier and productive lifestyle.

What Are the Takeaways From This Chapter?

As an innovation leader committed to high-quality education that provides opportunities for all students to navigate a path to success, you can see CBE in action in many districts across the United States and the world. There are classrooms where students set their own learning objectives and develop the skills they will need in their future through authentic learning activities. Students collaborate with others both in real time and virtually to solve real problems that matter to them. Students learn anywhere, anytime, and any way because technology is ubiquitous in their journey and essential in preparing them for an ever-changing future. Students are customizing their own learning and using both virtual and real-time events to deepen their knowledge. Technology supports academic learning and also assists with monitoring emotional, social, and physical needs. CBE offers the learning map, and technology assists in the learning activities and progress monitoring. There are many pockets of excellence and educational leaders ready to share their experiences of transforming systems from traditional to CBE with colleagues.

EPILOGUE

There is a wealth of information already published from others who recognize the need to change our education system. Again, just tinkering with an already broken system will never get us there. We need major transformation of an existing system that continues to mirror the factory model of learning. This major transition should be both systemic and systematic, meaning you have to look at the entire system and examine everything that exists and be willing to make difficult decisions for the good of all students. CBE is such an approach because you reset the entire curriculum and how you teach, assess, and report students' progress to better meet their needs. Plus, it's important that we adopt a systematic approach so we continue to use data to measure our progress and continue to innovate to achieve the desired results. Finally, every decision we make should include putting the student at the center of the system and committing ourselves to ensure every student is better equipped with the skills to thrive in the future.

CBE in isolation is not the sole solution to remedy an ailing education system, but it is a key ingredient to help us all get on the same page about what it is we are trying to teach and what it is we want our students to be learning. This road map of learning is the critical first step. This clarity rarely exists within our current schools. Teachers will continue to wing it in isolation until there is a guaranteed and viable curriculum; the CBE approach allows this to happen.

We have shared with you the current condition of our schools, our solution, and how this journey will change your role. The ultimate goal for writing this book is to scale the work we initiated in 2001. We want to help all stakeholder groups but especially want to give leaders more confidence with the skills and processes to begin their journey. The genesis of CBE Ignited is rooted in decades of successful implementation of actual classroom teachers, school principals, and district superintendents. Before CBE Ignited begins a long-term commitment to partner with any school or district, the process begins with a request for an on-site review to see if the district exhibits the readiness culture to move forward. Depending on the size of the organization, we can spend anywhere from one day to several weeks meeting with all stakeholder groups, including students, to determine their readiness to seriously begin this journey.

An extensive set of resources and tools is available on the CBEIgnited.org website. We bring our experiences to help guide and support anyone who sees the value of this approach and would like more support. We provide clear road maps of what this journey entails, including trainings, tools, and resources for educators. Remember this is a journey, and sometimes just taking the first step is the hardest. There are thousands of educators at every level increasing student success through a CBE system, and we hope to be the accelerator of inviting many more.

CBE will transform the educational landscape in the future. CBE Ignited extends an invitation to you to join a revolution that will make a difference for every student and everyone's future success.

APPENDIX A

List of CBE Implemented Locations

The CBE Ignited process proposes a systemwide change from time-bound to student-centered, performance-based learning. The following three districts have successfully reached the replication phase.

Westminster Public Schools
6933 Raleigh Street
Westminster, CO 80030

Lindsay Unified School District
371 E. Hermosa Street
Lindsay, CA 93247

Chugach School District
9312 Vanguard Drive, Suite 100
Anchorage, AK 99507

The following sections list schools and districts, and charter schools and networks that self-proclaim as implementing CBE, but we have not verified where they are on the road map.

School Districts and Schools

- Dallas Independent School District, Texas: Serving 230 schools
- Eastern Carver County Schools, Minnesota: Serving 18 schools
- Henry County Schools, Georgia: Serving 50 schools
- Kettle Moraine School District, Wisconsin: Serving 10 schools
- Mesa Public Schools, Arizona: Serving 87 schools
- Mesa County Valley School District 51, Arizona: Serving 46 schools

- Montpelier Public Schools, Vermont: Serving 3 schools
- Noble Public Schools, Oklahoma: Serving 5 schools
- Pinellas County Schools, Florida: Serving 140 schools
- Kennebec Intra-District Schools, Maine: Serving 9 schools
- Sanborn Regional School District, New Hampshire: Serving 4 schools

Charter Schools and Networks

- Aveson Global Leadership Academy, California: Enrolls about 415 students
- Big Picture Learning: A network of schools in 25 states
- Blackstone Academy Charter School, Rhode Island: Enrolls about 300 students
- Boston Day and Evening Academy, Massachusetts: Enrolls about 400 students
- Brooklyn Laboratory Charter School, New York: Enrolls about 325 students
- Crosstown High, Tennessee: Enrolls about 500 students
- Furr High School, an Institute for Innovative Thinking, Texas: Enrolls about 1,010 students
- Level Up Academy, Minnesota: Enrolls about 150 students
- Making Community Connections Charter School, New Hampshire: Network of 2 schools
- Summit Public Schools, California/Washington: Network of 11 schools
- Urban Assembly Maker Academy, New York: Enrolls about 100 students

APPENDIX B

Glossary of Terms

Artificial intelligence (AI). A simulation of human intelligence processes by machines, especially computer systems.

Assessment. Any type of measurement showing learner progress.

Bipartisan support. Encouragement for all areas of change being addressed, no matter the issue or stakeholder role.

Burning platform. Refers to a metaphor of a platform you are standing on that is burning up. You must make a choice to burn or jump off. For education, we use this term to show that a crisis can often be an opportunity for change. Unless the situation is dire, most choose not to change.

Competency-based education (CBE). Moving away from the traditional time-bound system to a learner-centered, performance-based system.

Culture. Can refer to specific traditions within a community or the overall feeling of a classroom, school, and district. For example, a culture of respect for everyone refers to all persons (learners, facilitators, administrators, parents, and community) agreeing to show respect to each other.

Curriculum. Set of instructions for learning in various content areas and grade levels; what students need to know and be able to do.

Feedback report. An on-site visit to measure the depth of implementation that comes with a report on findings and recommendations (usually directly to the leadership and/or administrative team).

Formative feedback. Results of assessments that help identify gaps in learning and verify strengths. This can be self-assessments, peer assessments or feedback, teacher-driven assessments, or any type of constructive criticism that enables the learner to improve.

High-stakes test. Assessment that relates outcome to specific movement.

Learning management system (LMS). A platform to assist all stakeholders in mapping out learners' guides toward their educational goals, allowing for tracking of progress from learners, facilitators, administrators, and other stakeholders.

Malcolm Baldrige award. The Malcolm Baldrige National Quality Award is an award established by the U.S. Congress in 1987 to raise awareness of quality management and recognize U.S. companies that have implemented successful quality management systems. The award is the nation's highest presidential honor for performance excellence.

National Assessment of Educational Progress (NAEP). Often called the Nation's Report Card; compares various subject areas among states, large urban districts, and various student groups.

National Center for Education Statistics (NCES). Collects, analyzes, and makes available data related to education in the United States and other nations.

No Child Left Behind (NCLB). National legislation mandating high-stakes testing.

Personal, social, and service learning. Learning with a focus on citizenship skills and personal and intrapersonal development.

Playlists. Options for completing learning.

Proficiency-based education. Education that requires mastery of specific targets.

Proficiency scale. Learning progression describing rigor (sometimes referred to as rubrics).

Proof of concept. Showing success in a whole system over time and change.

Science, technology, engineering, and mathematics (STEM) or science, technology, engineering, arts and culture, and mathematics (STEAM). Educational approach that encourages a holistic, interdisciplinary process of problem solving, collaboration, and critical thinking.

Scope and sequence. Curriculum that is mapped out in specific order with lesson plans.

Shared vision. Where the organization or district is headed toward; it must include input from all stakeholders to have buy-in and support.

Social-emotional learning. Developing skills to help understand and regulate emotions, manage intrapersonal skills and relationships, and practice self-awareness.

Stakeholder. Anyone with a vested interest (students, learners, teachers, facilitators, parents, board members, community members, administrators, policymakers, and so on).

Standards-based education. Education that maps learning toward specific targets.

Static delivery model. A model of teaching that doesn't change or adapt but continues the way it has always been done.

Student engagement. How excited students are about their learning.

Summative feedback. Results of assessments that show mastery of specific skills at very specific times.

Systemwide. Includes a whole district, not just one or a few schools.

Traditional education system. Learners are put into groupings by age and only allowed to progress at given times that fit the schedule of the organization.

Voice and choice. Term given to learners who are empowered to have a say in their own education; they are able to navigate their own learning (that does not mean they decide what they will learn; rather, it means that they are a part of the process for those decisions and understand the system and how to navigate it).

References and Resources

Alaska Department of Education and Early Development. (n.d.). *Alaska standards and instruction*. Accessed at https://education.alaska.gov/standards on December 6, 2023.

American Academy of Pediatrics. (2021, October 19). *AAP-AACAP-CHA declaration of a national emergency in child and adolescent mental health*. Accessed at www.aap.org/en/advocacy/child-and-adolescent-healthy-mental-development/aap-aacap-cha-declaration-of-a-national-emergency-in-child-and-adolescent-mental-health/ on January 3, 2024.

American University School of Education. (2021, February 16). *Addressing teacher burnout: Causes, symptoms, and strategies* [Blog post]. Accessed at https://soeonline.american.edu/blog/teacher-burnout/ on June 9, 2023.

Balfanz, R., & Legters, N. (2004). *Locating the dropout crisis: Which high schools produce the nation's dropouts? Where are they located? Who attends them?* Baltimore, MD: Johns Hopkins University Center for Research on the Education of Students Placed at Risk.

Barnum, M. (2023, March 6). *Teacher turnover hits new highs across the U.S.* Accessed at www.chalkbeat.org/2023/3/6/23624340/teacher-turnover-leaving-the-profession-quitting-higher-rate on June 9, 2023.

Bathina, J. (2011). *Among the groves: Lindsay lives*. Trenton, GA: BookLocker.

Belsha, K. (2021, September 27). *Stress and short tempers: Schools struggle with behavior as students return*. Accessed at www.chalkbeat.org/2021/9/27/22691601/student-behavior-stress-trauma-return on January 3, 2024.

Bergmann, J. (2022). *The mastery learning handbook: A competency-based approach to student achievement*. Alexandria, VA: ASCD.

Broder, D. S. (2002, April 14). *School success in strange places*. Accessed at www.washingtonpost.com/archive/opinions/2002/04/14/school-success-in-strange-places/542e97ed-0dc6-41e5-a9a7-f1b35f190e1c on May 22, 2023.

Brodersen, M. (2020, June 24). *Using competency-based education systems to measure student progress*. Accessed at www.marzanoresearch.com/using-competency-based-education-systems-to-measure-student-progress on January 29, 2024.

Brooks, D. (2023, February 16). *America should be in the middle of a schools revolution*. Accessed at www.nytimes.com/2023/02/16/opinion/america-schools-revolution.html on May 19, 2023.

Camera, L. (2023, June 21). *U.S. teens' reading and math scores feature largest declines ever.* Accessed at www.usnews.com/news/education-news/articles/2023-06-21/u-s-teens-reading-and-math-scores-feature-largest-declines-ever on February 12, 2024.

Center on Education Policy. (2020). *History and evolution of public education in the U.S.* Washington, DC: George Washington Graduate School of Education and Human Development.

Chen, G. (2023, February 22). *Why 82% of public schools are failing.* Accessed at www.publicschoolreview.com/blog/why-82-of-public-schools-are-failing on August 21, 2023.

Chouinard, Y. (2019). *Some stories: Lessons from the edge of business and sport.* Ventura, CA: Patagonia.

Day, J. C., & Newburger, E. C. (2002, July). *The big payoff: Educational attainment and synthetic estimates of work-life earnings* (Report no. P23-210). Washington, DC: U.S. Census Bureau.

Dee, T. S. (2022, November 2). *Public school enrollment is down by more than a million. Why?* Accessed at www.edweek.org/leadership/opinion-public-school-enrollment-is-down-by-more-than-a-million-why/2022/11 on June 9, 2023.

DeLorenzo, R. (2020, April 28). *Could Russia's 21st century Sputnik be in educational transformation?* Accessed at www.gettingsmart.com/2020/04/28/could-russias-21st-century-sputnik-be-in-educational-transformation on May 22, 2023.

DeLorenzo, R. A., Battino, W. J., Schreiber, R. M., & Gaddy Carrio, B. B. (2008). *Delivering on the promise: The education revolution.* Bloomington, IN: Solution Tree Press.

Diliberti, M. K., & Schwartz, H. L. (2023). *Educator turnover has markedly increased, but districts have taken actions to boost teacher ranks.* Accessed at www.rand.org/content/dam/rand/pubs/research_reports/RRA900/RRA956-14/RAND_RRA956-14.pdf on June 9, 2023.

DoSomething.org. (n.d.). *11 facts about high school dropout rates.* Accessed at www.dosomething.org/us/facts/11-facts-about-high-school-dropout-rates on May 18, 2023.

Duffy, F. M. (2002). *Step-up-to-excellence: An innovative approach into managing and rewarding performance in school systems.* Lanham, MD: Scarecrow Education.

Duffy, F. M., & Reigeluth, C. M. (2008). The school system transformation (SST) protocol. *Educational Technology, 48*(4), 41–49.

Dweck, C. S. (2016). *Mindset: The new psychology of success.* New York: Ballantine.

Eckert, J. (2021). *10 teacher picks for best tech tools.* Accessed at www.edutopia.org/article/10-teacher-picks-best-tech-tools/ on December 6, 2023.

European Commission. (2021, September 1). *Finland AI strategy report.* Accessed at https://ai-watch.ec.europa.eu/countries/finland/finland-ai-strategy-report_en on January 3, 2024.

Evans, C. M., Landl, E., & Thompson, J. (2021). *Making sense of K–12 competency-based education: A systematic literature review of implementation and outcomes research from 2000 to 2019.* Accessed at https://onlinelibrary.wiley.com/doi/full/10.1002/cbe2.1228 on January 4, 2024.

FactsMaps. (n.d.). *PISA 2018 worldwide ranking—Average score of mathematics, science and reading.* Accessed at https://factsmaps.com/pisa-2018-worldwide-ranking-average-score-of-mathematics-science-reading on August 21, 2023.

Fredin, A., Fuchsteiner, P., & Portz, K. (2015). Working toward more engaged and successful accounting students: A balanced scorecard approach. *American Journal of Business Education, 8*(1), 49–62.

Fullan, M. (2003). *Change forces with a vengeance.* New York: Routledge.

Gagnon, L. (2023, May 31). *Competency-based education across America.* Accessed at https://aurora-institute.org/cw_post/competency-based-education-across-america/ on February 14, 2024.

Gewertz, C. (2018, April 2). *How high school diploma requirements fall short of college admission standards.* Accessed at www.edweek.org/teaching-learning/how-high-school-diploma-requirements-fall-short-of-college-admission-standards/2018/04 on August 21, 2023.

Goldstein, D. (2019). *It just isn't working: PISA test scores cast doubt on U.S. education efforts.* Accessed at www.nytimes.com/2019/12/03/us/us-students-international-test-scores.html on May 18, 2023.

Goldstein, D. (2022, January 3). *"It's chaos" as schools confront Omicron.* Accessed at www.nytimes.com/2022/01/03/us/school-reopening-classrooms-omicron.html on January 3, 2024.

Gradient Learning. (2023). *Gradient learning poll: Student engagement.* Accessed at https://gradientlearning.go-vip.net/gradientlearningwebsite/wp-content/uploads/sites/2/2023/01/GradientLearningPoll_StudentEngagement.pdf on June 8, 2023.

Hall, S., Schmautzer, D., Tmiri, S., Ibrahim, H., Dorn, E., & Sarfraz, S. (2023). *The skills revolution and the future of learning and earning.* Accessed at www.mckinsey.com/~/media/mckinsey/industries/education/our%20insights/the%20skills%20revolution%20and%20the%20future%20of%20learning%20and%20earning/the-skills-revolution-and-the-future-of-learning-and-earning-report-f.pdf on August 22, 2023.

Hasso Plattner Institute of Design at Stanford. (2012). *An introduction to design thinking process guide.* Stanford, CA: Author.

Hattie, J., & Zierer, K. (2017). *10 mindframes for visible learning: Teaching for success.* London: Routledge.

Haynes, E., Zeiser, K., Surr, W., Hauser, A., Clymer, L., Walston, J., et al. (2016). *Looking under the hood of competency-based education: The relationship between competency-based practices and students' learning skills, behaviors, and dispositions.* Accessed at www.air.org/sites/default/files/downloads/report/CBE-Study%20Full%20Report.pdf on August 21, 2023.

Haystead, M. W. (2010, April). *RISC vs. non-RISC schools: A comparison of student proficiencies for reading, writing, and mathematics.* Denver, CO: Marzano Resources.

Henebery, B. (2023, February 20). *Landmark study reveals number one factor impacting student learning.* Accessed at www.theeducatoronline.com/k12/news/landmark-study-reveals-number-one-factor-impacting-student-learning/281967 on January 9, 2024.

Hersey, P., Blanchard, K. H., & Johnson, D. E. (2013). *Management of organizational behavior: Leading human resources* (10th ed.). New York: Pearson.

Horn, M. B. (2022). *From reopen to reinvent: Recreating school for every child.* Hoboken, NJ: Jossey-Bass.

Hunter, R. (2004). *Madeline Hunter's mastery teaching: Increasing instructional effectiveness in elementary and secondary schools.* Thousand Oaks, CA: Corwin Press.

International Society for Technology in Education. (1998). *National education technology standards for students.* Washington, DC: Author.

Investment to the Future. (n.d.a). *Personality potential development program.* Accessed at https://vbudushee.ru/en/modern-education/personal-potential-development-program on January 4, 2024.

Investment to the Future. (n.d.b). *Research consortium of universities "personality potential development in education."* Accessed at https://vbudushee.ru/en/modern-education/research-consortium-of-universities-personal-potential-development-in-education/ on January 4, 2024.

Jacobson, L. (2022, October 17). *Analysis: States to "likely see a doubling" of pre-pandemic chronic absenteeism.* Accessed at www.the74million.org/article/analysis-states-to-likely-see-a-doubling-of-pre-pandemic-chronic-absenteeism on June 9, 2023.

Joseph, D. (2013, November 11). *Leadership capacity for second-order change.* Accessed at https://aurora-institute.org/cw_post/leadership-capacity-for-second-order-change/ on January 4, 2024.

Khan, A., Khan, S., Zia-Ul-Islam, S., & Han, M. (2017). Communication skills of a teacher and its role in the development of the students' academic success. *Journal of Education and Practice, 8*(1), 18–21.

Kuhfeld, M., Soland, J., Lewis, K., & Morton, E. (2022, March 3). *The pandemic has had devastating impacts on learning. What will it take to help students catch up?* Accessed at www.brookings.edu/blog/brown-center-chalkboard/2022/03/03/the-pandemic-has-had-devastating-impacts-on-learning-what-will-it-take-to-help-students-catch-up on June 9, 2023.

Laderer, A. (2023, March 1). *Gen Z's mental health crisis and collective trauma.* Accessed at www.charliehealth.com/post/gen-zs-mental-health-crisis-collective-trauma on December 4, 2023.

Lake, R., & Pillow, T. (2022, November 1). *The alarming state of the American student in 2022.* Accessed at www.brookings.edu/blog/brown-center-chalkboard/2022/11/01/the-alarming-state-of-the-american-student-in-2022 on August 22, 2023.

Leonhardt, D. (2022). *No way to grow up*. Accessed at www.nytimes.com/2022/01/04/briefing/american-children-crisis-pandemic.html on May 18, 2023.

Levinson, M., & Markovits, D. (2022, June 23). *The biggest disruption in the history of American education*. Accessed at www.theatlantic.com/ideas/archive/2022/06/covid-learning-loss-remote-school/661360 on May 18, 2023.

Lewis, K., Kuhfeld, M., Ruzek, E., & McEachin, A. (2021, July). *Learning during COVID-19: Reading and math achievement in the 2020-21 school year*. Accessed at www.nwea.org/uploads/2021/07/Learning-during-COVID-19-Reading-and-math-achievement-in-the-2020-2021-school-year.research-brief-1.pdf on January 3, 2024.

Lezotte, L. W. (1997). *Learning for all*. Webberville, MI: Effective Schools Products.

Lindsay Unified. (2023, December 11). *The history of Lindsay Unified School District* [Video file]. Accessed at www.youtube.com/watch?v=usTgRMEcAUQ on January 9, 2024.

Lindsay Unified School District. (2017). *Beyond reform: Systemic shifts toward personalized learning*. Bloomington, IN: Marzano Resources.

Low, A. (2020, May 6). *T3 Alliance: Turning a crisis into an educational opportunity*. Accessed at www.gettingsmart.com/2020/05/06/t3-alliance-turning-a-crisis-into-an-educational-opportunity on June 20, 2023.

Ly, L. (2023, May 4). *Test scores for 8-grade students decline in US history and civics following prior declines in math and reading, report says*. Accessed at www.cnn.com/2023/05/04/us/nations-report-card-us-history-civics/index.html on August 21, 2023.

Lynch, M. (2016, February 18). *3 unusual statistics about the U.S. educational system*. Accessed at www.theedadvocate.org/3-unusual-statistics-about-the-u-s-educational-system/ on August 21, 2023.

MacGillis, A. (2023, June 19). *Can America's students recover what they lost during the pandemic?* Accessed at www.propublica.org/article/pandemic-covid-education-test-scores-schools-students on August 22, 2023.

Mahnken, K. (2018, July 2). *Education by the numbers: 9 statistics that have made us think differently about America's schools this academic year*. Accessed at www.the74million.org/education-by-the-numbers-9-statistics-that-have-made-us-think-differently-about-americas-schools-this-academic-year/ on August 22, 2023.

Marzano, R. J., & Abbott, S. D. (2022). *Teaching in a competency-based elementary school*. Bloomington, IN: Marzano Resources.

Marzano, R. J., Aschoff, A. S., & Avila, A. (2022). *Teaching in a competency-based secondary school*. Bloomington, IN: Marzano Resources.

Marzano, R. J., & Kendall, J. S. (1996). *A comprehensive guide to designing standards-based districts, schools, and classrooms*. Alexandria, VA: ASCD.

Marzano, R. J., Kosena, B. J., & Hubbs, B. (2022). *Leading a competency-based elementary school*. Bloomington, IN: Marzano Research.

Marzano, R. J., Norford, J. S., Finn, M., & Finn, D., III. (2017). *A handbook for personalized competency-based education.* Bloomington, IN: Marzano Research.

Marzano, R. J., Waters, T., & McNulty, B. A. (2005). *School leadership that works: From research to results.* Alexandria, VA: ASCD.

Matthews, A. L. (2023, December 19). *School shootings in the US: Fast facts.* Accessed at www.cnn.com/2023/09/22/us/school-shootings-fast-facts-dg/index.html on January 3, 2024.

Mervosh, S. (2022, September 1). *The pandemic erased two decades of progress in math and reading.* Accessed at www.nytimes.com/2022/09/01/us/national-test-scores-math-reading-pandemic.html on June 9, 2023.

Mourant, R. (2011). *Tools and online courses for Alaskan educators.* Alaska's Learning Network (AKLN). Alaska Department of Education and Early Development.

Muhammad, A. (2017). *Transforming school culture: How to overcome staff division* (2nd ed.). Bloomington, IN: Solution Tree Press.

National Center for Education Statistics. (n.d.a). *NAEP report card: 2022 NAEP mathematics assessment.* Accessed at www.nationsreportcard.gov/highlights/mathematics/2022/ on May 18, 2023.

National Center for Education Statistics. (n.d.b). *NAEP report card: 2022 NAEP reading assessment.* Accessed at www.nationsreportcard.gov/highlights/reading/2022/ on May 18, 2023.

National Center for Education Statistics. (2022, July 6). *More than 80 percent of U.S. public schools report pandemic has negatively impacted student behavior and socio-emotional development.* Accessed at https://nces.ed.gov/whatsnew/press_releases/07_06_2022.asp on June 9, 2023.

National Center for Education Statistics. (2023). *Status dropout rates.* Accessed at https://nces.ed.gov/programs/coe/indicator/coj on February 12, 2024.

National Commission on Excellence in Education. (1983, April). *A nation at risk: The imperative for educational reform.* Washington, DC: U.S. Government Printing Office.

National Institute of Standards and Technology. (n.d.). *Chugach School District: Malcolm Baldrige National Quality Award 2001 recipient, education.* Accessed at www.nist.gov/baldrige/chugach-school-district on August 22, 2023.

Norman, A. (2017, March 8). *The automation upheaval won't be limited to blue-collar jobs: Your job probably isn't robot-proof.* Accessed at https://futurism.com/the-automation-upheaval-wont-be-limited-to-blue-collar-jobs on June 9, 2023.

Obeng, K. (2020, October 1). *This rural California school district won $10K for students after innovating amid COVID-19.* Accessed at www.visaliatimesdelta.com/story/news/2020/10/01/lindsay-unified-wins-10-k-students-after-innovating-amid-covid-19/5883154002/ on January 4, 2024.

Organisation for Economic Co-operation and Development. (2010). *Strong performers and successful reformers in education: Lessons from PISA for the United States.* Accessed at www.oecd.org/pisa/pisaproducts/46581035.pdf on June 9, 2023.

Organisation for Economic Co-operation and Development. (2012). *Equity and quality in education: Supporting disadvantaged students and schools.* Accessed at www.oecd-ilibrary.org/education/equity-and-quality-in-education_9789264130852-en on February 13, 2024.

Organisation for Economic Co-operation and Development. (2019). *PISA 2018 results.* Accessed at www.oecd.org/pisa/publications/pisa-2018-results.htm on May 19, 2023.

Parsons, C. (2011, March 9). *82% of U.S. public schools could fail "No Child Left Behind" review, Obama administration says.* Accessed at www.latimes.com/archives/la-xpm-2011-mar-09-la-pn-obama-schools-20110310-story.html on August 21, 2023.

Reigeluth, C. M., & Karnopp, J. R. (2013). *Reinventing schools: It's time to break the mold.* Lanham, MD: Rowman & Littlefield.

Rix, K. (2023, March 22). *Competency-based education: What it is and how it can boost student engagement.* Accessed at www.usnews.com/education/k12/articles/competency-based-education-what-it-is-and-how-it-can-boost-student-engagement on January 4, 2024.

Ruyle, M., Child, L., & Dome, N. (2022). *School wellness wheel: A framework addressing trauma, culture, and mastery to raise student achievement.* Bloomington, IN: Marzano Resources.

Schreiber, R., & Battino, W. (2002). *A guide to reinventing schools.* Anchorage, AK: Chugach School District.

Senge, P. M. (1990). *The fifth discipline: The art and practice of the learning organization.* New York: Doubleday.

Sjøen, M. M. (2013). *From global competition to intercultural competence: What teacher-training students with cross-cultural teaching experience should be learning.* Trondheim, Norway: Department of Teacher Education, Norwegian University of Science and Technology.

Sommer, B. (2020, April 9). *Learning and loving are not cancelled at Lindsay Unified: Anywhere/anytime learning—Lindsay Unified School District's response to COVID-19.* Accessed at https://medium.com/@Lindsay_USD/learning-and-loving-are-not-cancelled-at-lindsay-unified-anywhere-anytime-learning-lindsay-da592155f9c6 on January 4, 2024.

Sparks, S. D. (2022, October 24). *Two decades of progress, nearly gone: National math, reading scores hit historic lows.* Accessed at www.edweek.org/leadership/two-decades-of-progress-nearly-gone-national-math-reading-scores-hit-historic-lows/2022/10 on June 9, 2023.

Stevens, K. B. (2020, September 21). *Still left behind: How America's schools keep failing our children.* Accessed at www.aei.org/research-products/report/still-left-behind/ on August 21, 2023.

Stoll, C., & Giddings, G. (2015). *Reawakening the learner.* Lanham, MD: Rowman & Littlefield.

Subramony, D., Molenda, M., Betrus, A., & Thalheimer, W. (2014). The mythical retention chart and the corruption of Dale's cone of experience. *Educational Technology, 54*(6), 6–16.

Sudderth, A. (n.d.). *What is student centered learning and why is it important?* Accessed at https://xqsuperschool.org/teaching-learning/what-is-student-centered-learning/ on August 21, 2023.

TEDx Talks. (2011, August 5). *TEDxDesMoines—Angela Maiers—You matter* [Video file]. Accessed at www.youtube.com/watch?v=7FHdHUzRnms&ab_channel=TEDxTalks on December 4, 2023.

Wilbur, T. G., & Roscigno, V. J. (2016). *First-generation disadvantage and college enrollment/completion.* Accessed at https://journals.sagepub.com/doi/10.1177/2378023116664351 on January 9, 2024.

Williams, L. (2023, February 2). *The military-industrial history of American public education.* Accessed at https://rebeleducator.co/the-military-industrial-history-of-american-public-education/ on August 21, 2023.

Wood, J. H., & Robinson, G. (2021, November 12). *Schools in crisis: Here's how we can fix education in America and ensure our kids succeed.* Accessed at www.usatoday.com/story/opinion/2021/11/12/covid-opportunity-transform-education/6368001001/ on August 22, 2023.

XQ Institute. (n.d.). *Are high schools preparing students for the future?* Accessed at https://xqsuperschool.org/reports/are-high-schools-preparing-students-for-the-future on June 9, 2023.

Yard, E., Radhakrishnan, L., Ballesteros, M. F., Sheppard, M., Gates, A., Stein, Z., et al. (2021, June 18). *Emergency department visits for suspected suicide attempts among persons aged 12–25 years before and during the COVID-19 pandemic—United States, January 2019–May 2021.* Accessed at www.cdc.gov/mmwr/volumes/70/wr/mm7024e1.htm on January 3, 2024.

Index

Unpacking the Competency-Based Classroom
Jonathan G. Vander Els and Brian M. Stack
Explore a variety of perspectives and examples from educators who have shifted to CBE with great results. The book details how to do the work by reevaluating and revamping traditional policies, structures, and procedures, including assessment and instruction practices.
BKG018

Scheduling for Personalized Competency-Based Education
Douglas Finn III and Michelle Finn
A challenge at the heart of personalized competency-based education (PCBE) is grouping and scheduling students according to their learning needs rather than their age. With this guidebook, you'll take a deep dive into the why and how of these foundational PCBE components.
BKL049

Beyond Reform
Lindsay Unified School District
Learn how Lindsay Unified School District took action to improve student learning by shifting from a traditional time-based education system to a learner-centered performance-based system. By adopting and tailoring Lindsay Unified's instructional model, you and your team can embark on your own district's transformation.
BKL036

The Marzano Academies Model Series
Robert J. Marzano, Seth D. Abbott, Alexander S. Aschoff, Ashley Avila, Brian J. Kosena, Patrick B. Hardy
A blueprint for success with competency-based education from experts and educators who have done this work. Leaders and teachers at the elementary and secondary levels will gain innovative, equitable, and effective practices for schools and classrooms.
BKL053, BKL054, BKL055, BKL056

Solution Tree | Press
a division of Solution Tree

Visit SolutionTree.com or call 800.733.6786 to order.